"Finally, a book that single women can relate to! Too often, self-help books operate on fear-mongering—aiming to convince women that they have some major defect preventing them from finding Mr. Right and they better fix it. Michelle Cove starts with the assumption that single women are just fine as they are and then provides warm, friendly, and wise advice to help women be their happiest selves, no matter what stage of being single they are in."

—COURTNEY E. MARTIN, EDITOR, FEMINISTING.COM, AND AUTHOR OF *Perfect Girls, Starving Daughters: How the Quest for Perfection Is Harming Young Women*

"This book is for every woman who's single and been told to rush toward the altar, but who knows that her life—her own precious, dynamic, exciting, life—is full and worthwhile. This book is an affirmation that no woman should settle for less than she deserves. It's a toast to all the young women who know they deserve everything they want, and it reminds them that they shouldn't settle for less—not in friends, not in careers, and certainly not in romantic partners. Michelle Cove is a storyteller, helping women script their own contemporary, sassy, happy endings."

—BETH JONES, COAUTHOR OF *Three Wishes: A True Story of Good Friends, Crushing Heartbreak, and Astonishing Luck on Our Way to Love and Motherhood*

"If the question is, Why are you still single? the answer can be found in this book. Michelle Cove has created a boot camp for single women who need a reminder that they are islands of sanity in an insane world—not the other way around. Every woman will relate to at least one of the real-life stories. It should be required reading for women over thirty who are tired of feeling pressure to marry. Give it as a gift to your married friends and family who have forgotten what it's like to be single, since they keep asking, When are you gonna get married?"

—LARA DYAN, COHOST OF *ChickChat*

"While so many books on the market for single women try to teach readers how to make men love them, this is a book that gives women the steps to help them genuinely love themselves. Better yet, Michelle Cove offers these steps in a friendly, compassionate, even humorous tone so it feels like spending time with your wisest best friend."

—JOSIE BROWN, EDITOR, SINGLEMINDEDWOMEN.COM, AND COAUTHOR OF *The Complete Idiot's Guide to Finding Mr. Right*

"Michelle Cove delivers. In the opening pages of her book, she says her book will not help the single woman fall in love. Instead she offers strategies for creating lasting love. Her book brims with action plans that enable a woman to 'use her inner voice.' Cove believes in joy and balance, not stress and relentless pursuit. I happen to be married and yet the book spoke to me as well. It's a wake-up call for all women (all people?) to get back in touch with what makes them wonderful, what makes them worth marrying in the first place."

—SHULAMIT REINHARZ, FOUNDER AND DIRECTOR,
  WOMEN'S STUDIES RESEARCH CENTER AND HADASSAH-BRANDEIS INSTITUTE

"Cove talks as if she's sitting over coffee with you in the kitchen, urging you to listen to your inner voice as well as offering good solid advice—advice you'll want, regardless your shade of single."

—DR. KAREN GAIL LEWIS, AUTHOR OF *With or Without a Man:*
  Single Women Taking Control of Their Lives

"What I love so much about this book is its friendly but no-nonsense approach to what it's like being single today, and how much better life can be with just a tweak of your mind-set. Michelle Cove's steps are so specific and easy to use that right away readers will learn to tune out the outside voices questioning them, and readers will feel truly empowered. This is a book that will inspire single women of all ages to take charge of their lives!"

—KERRY DAVID, AWARD-WINNING PRODUCER OF *Seeking Happily Ever After* AND
  My Date with Drew

SEEKING
HAPPILY
EVER AFTER

MICHELLE COVE

JEREMY P. TARCHER/PENGUIN

a member of Penguin Group (USA) Inc.

New York

SEEKING
HAPPILY
EVER AFTER

Navigating the Ups and Downs

of Being Single

Without Losing Your Mind

(And Finding Lasting Love Along the Way)

JEREMY P. TARCHER/PENGUIN
Published by the Penguin Group
Penguin Group (USA) Inc., 375 Hudson Street, New York, New York 10014, USA ·
Penguin Group (Canada), 90 Eglinton Avenue East, Suite 700, Toronto, Ontario M4P 2Y3,
Canada (a division of Pearson Penguin Canada Inc.) · Penguin Books Ltd, 80 Strand,
London WC2R 0RL, England · Penguin Ireland, 25 St Stephen's Green, Dublin 2, Ireland
(a division of Penguin Books Ltd) · Penguin Group (Australia), 250 Camberwell Road,
Camberwell, Victoria 3124, Australia (a division of Pearson Australia Group Pty Ltd) ·
Penguin Books India Pvt Ltd, 11 Community Centre, Panchsheel Park, New Delhi–110 017,
India · Penguin Group (NZ), 67 Apollo Drive, Rosedale, North Shore 0632,
New Zealand (a division of Pearson New Zealand Ltd) · Penguin Books (South Africa)
(Pty) Ltd, 24 Sturdee Avenue, Rosebank, Johannesburg 2196, South Africa

Penguin Books Ltd, Registered Offices: 80 Strand, London WC2R 0RL, England

Most Tarcher/Penguin books are available at special quantity discounts for bulk purchase for sales
promotions, premiums, fund-raising, and educational needs. Special books or book excerpts
also can be created to fit specific needs. For details, write Penguin Group (USA) Inc.
Special Markets, 375 Hudson Street, New York, NY 10014.

Library of Congress Cataloging-in-Publication Data

Cove, Michelle.
Seeking happily ever after : navigating the ups and downs of being single
without losing your mind (and finding lasting love along the way) / Michelle Cove.
p.   cm.
ISBN 978-1-58542-831-1
1. Single women—Life-skills guides.   I. Title.
HQ800.2.C698   2010   2010023994
646.7'7082—dc22

Printed in the United States of America
1 3 5 7 9 10 8 6 4 2

Book design by Meighan Cavanaugh

Neither the publisher nor the author is engaged in rendering professional advice or services
to the individual reader. The ideas, procedures, and suggestions contained in this book
are not intended as a substitute for consulting with a physician. All matters regarding your health
require medical supervision. Neither the author nor the publisher shall be liable or responsible
for any loss or damage allegedly arising from any information or suggestion in this book.

While the author has made every effort to provide accurate telephone numbers and
Internet addresses at the time of publication, neither the publisher nor the author
assumes any responsibility for errors, or for changes that occur after publication.
Further, the publisher does not have any control over and does not assume
any responsibility for author or third-party websites or their content.

For the bold single women who trusted me with

their personal stories and allowed me to

share these stories for the greater good . . .

CONTENTS

PART THREE

Changing Love-Life Goals

This map is all confusing! I used to be certain of my destination, but now, after a few twists and turns, I seem to be on a whole new path.

PART FOUR

Navigating a Marriage-Obsessed Culture

Time-out, people. Who decided this was a race, and what's the *&#^ing rush?

SEEKING HAPPILY EVER AFTER

Introduction

What single woman hasn't been made to feel like she is a social screwup? According to a 2007 *New York Times* article, 51 percent of women are single—and yet somehow being unmarried is still considered an oddball lifestyle. If you're like most singles, you've been bombarded with questions like, "How long have you been alone?" and "Are you doing that online dating?" and "Why is someone as great as you still not married?" The message is clear: There is something wrong with you, and you'd better fix it.

On vulnerable days, it's easy to buy into the idea that you have a major defect. After all, it sure seems easy for billions of other women around the world to get hitched and have babies. You're a bright, lovely person. Why not you? On other days, the commentary seems ridiculous, and you feel secure knowing you didn't settle for the wrong guy. "Sure, I'd like to find someone," you think, "but there is nothing wrong with me." Heck, maybe you don't even want to marry.

How confident you feel may depend on the day. There are times when you appreciate the upsides of being single: You get to choose how you want to live without major compromise; you don't have to check in with anyone if you're enjoying yourself and want to stay out longer; you don't need permission before making vacation plans or spending money however you see fit. There is the thrill and endorphin rush of that first kiss that most married people will never experience again. Oh, and there's the joy of walking past screaming babies in strollers and knowing you don't have to deal with that.

Then there are days when you wonder if you will ever find the right person, or whether the guy you're currently with is him. If you're not dating, there are moments of loneliness, cravings for intimacy (or flat-out sex), maybe fear of what a life without marriage looks like, and an urge to feel more settled. If you are dating, or even committed, you may have doubts about whether you picked the right guy and/or what kind of relationship you want with him.

You know from listening to your married friends that it's not perfect on their side of the fence (they tell you routinely how lucky you are that you get to focus on yourself). But what's clear is that married folks, content or not, are on the *right* side of the fence, the one that proves they are "normal." We live in a culture where the wedding is the finish line. If that's true, you're falling behind.

EVERYBODY'S FAVORITE PET PROJECT

Having married in my thirties, I've lived on both sides of the fence. As a single woman, I found my life was frequently considered a puzzle for others to solve. Strangers sitting next to me on the plane or at a dinner party would ask, "Are you married?" When I'd say no, the onslaught would begin: "My closest friend was single for the longest time, but then she met someone on Match.com and she couldn't be happier!" or "I have a second cousin in Kentucky who I think is single and I'm going to tell him about you," or "My mother's sister waited too long to think about marriage and now she's alone—it's so sad."

Well, that is extremely helpful, thank you.

I remember being told by a colleague that the online dating sites I picked "sucked" and that was why I couldn't find anyone. Huh? What does that even mean? There were friends and relatives who would hug me hello while asking, "Are you dating anyone?" My relationship status was endlessly fascinating, whether I was dating or not. It was like being transported back to seventh grade again where the topic of boys reigns supreme. Because of this obsessive focus, I didn't know who to talk to about my mixed feelings around being single: Who should I have called when I was feeling lonely? Or when I was feeling deflated from the stack of wedding invites from friends that kept arriving in my mailbox? Or when I needed someone to remind me there was more to life than whether I checked "single" or "in a relationship" on official forms?

I was nervous about voicing my concerns to single friends, especially since my status was often in flux. Those in the same boat would reply, "At least you're dating someone," or "Don't worry. I'm sure you'll get back together," or "What do you mean, you're not sure if he's the one?" Turning to the married people I knew wasn't the answer, either. If I mentioned the downsides of being single, they would roll their eyes and say, "You don't know how good you have it!" or offer pat reassurances: "When the right one comes along, you'll know," and "You'll find him when and where you least expect it."

Seriously?

I craved someone who could understand and validate what I was going through—a wise soul to assure me my feelings were normal and transitory. Better yet, I wanted someone to give me realistic ways of handling the numerous buttinskies who kept pressuring me to meet a guy; I yearned for ideas that would make me feel good during my single years, and not just endure the experience. Where was this wise soul? If she didn't exist, maybe there was a book that could help?

The book I longed for

Nope—there was nothing helpful on the book front. Strolling the aisles of the relationship section of bookstores was (and remains) a full-on assault: *He's Just Not That into You!* . . . *How to Avoid the*

10 Mistakes Single Women Make . . . Living Single: One Day at a Time . . . On My Own: The Art of Being a Woman Alone. The basic message: You're alone because you keep messing up, and/or you're going to end up alone, so you'd better get used to it.

This is so NOT what single women need to hear.

In large part, this book is the one I longed for during my own single years. I wanted a book that would reassure me that I was fine *married or not.* It would lift me up and open possibilities, not scare me into following a ten-step plan to grab the gold ring. Nor was I interested in self-help books insisting I would never find the love of my life, so I better make peace with being alone forever. I don't think so! I wanted an all-encompassing guide to help me feel strong and make wise choices in my love life regardless of whether I was hungering for a relationship, in one that raised doubts, or taking a breather from romance.

Unlike most relationship reads, this book operates on the assumption that "happily ever after" comes in different flavors: questioning marriage, rejecting it, or hoping for a wedding ring now or at some point. We are taught so early (thanks, Disney) that "happily ever after" means being saved by a prince who rescues a young woman and marries her quickly. Life just doesn't look like that; even for those pursuing marriage, the path to the altar today is rarely a straight walk down the aisle. Many women focus on their education and/or career before saying "I do," or live with a man for longer before marriage, or take time to travel and indulge in adventures. Single women may be seeking love, but they are not sitting around twiddling their thumbs.

Here's the thing: Until you know your own needs, the quest for fulfillment is useless. Forget about what the guy wants. What do *you* want? There are so many relationship books filled with "surefire" rules for making a man want you. (The rules include: "Don't call him back." "Never call a guy first." "Flirt, but don't be too flirty.") This book will help you determine what feels right for you, as well as what type of relationship will make you feel your best. As an added bonus, it turns out that healthy men want to be with women who know what they want.

This book will also shed light on the pressures and fears you and your single friends face. Too often our inner lives as single women are isolated from one another, leaving us feeling alone and misunderstood. This book will illuminate the ups and downs your friends may face in their love lives. By understanding one another, you can offer better support. Share appropriate sections with your mother, sibling, peers, or anyone else who could stand to learn a thing or two about not making you feel "less than" because you're unmarried. People say awful things to singles out of ignorance, with no understanding of the damage they inflict. Mark sections you'd like the person to read, with a note saying, "Let's discuss once you're done."

How will you *know* you're on the right path?

Most women I know call their close friends when they're having self-doubts. (Some of the things they wonder about: "Will I ever find someone?" "Do you think I'm giving up if I stop online dating?" "I just don't know if I'm with the right guy.") Although friends can be wonderful sounding boards, we forget that we are the best-equipped to give advice to ourselves. That's because few of us ever learn about tuning in to our *inner voice*, the single most valuable tool we possess. Your inner voice (which I realize sounds a little formal) is your true self that knows when things feel right or wrong. It is your internal compass that shows you where you are at all times. We all have one, but we can't take advantage of it until we learn how to use it. By the time you finish reading this book, you will know how.

Here's an example of how your inner voice can be helpful. Take loneliness. Many of us are led to believe that being lonely is shameful and should be avoided. If you tell someone you're lonely, he or she will likely tell you distracting stories, cheer you up with jokes, or suggest a night on the town so you forget about it. While this may be a good temporary fix, you will likely feel lonely again as soon as you're not distracted. The more you try to deny the feeling, the more anxious and maybe even hopeless you will feel. *Or* you can choose to tune in to your inner voice, which will tell you, "I feel lonely," so you can deal with it directly. Maybe the simple act of acknowledging and allowing yourself to feel your loneliness will be enough; perhaps you'll need to cry for twenty minutes before feeling better; maybe you'll write about it in your journal; or you might make plans to join a community so you're not so isolated. The point is, you can't get emotional relief or create a plan of action without first listening to your inner voice.

In every chapter, you will find a "tune in to your inner voice" exercise with a specific question to focus on about dating or your current relationship. Sit in a quiet place, close your eyes, and see what feelings come up when you ask the question (yes, this is the same as meditating). It's normal if you find yourself thinking, "I'm hungry," or "Is it cold in here?" or "What am I doing again?" Just allow those thoughts to surface and float away like bubbles, so you can get back to the question. In addition to these exercises, I strongly suggest spending at least ten minutes a day tuning in to your inner voice without any guided question other than, "How am I feeling right now?" If after a couple of weeks you're still struggling to access your inner voice, spend those ten minutes writing in a journal. The action of writing will likely make accessing your feelings easier because you'll feel less self-conscious than you would just sitting with your eyes closed. Don't worry about the quality or quantity of your writing; it's only for you. Eventually, you'll get to a place where you don't need the pen and paper anymore.

Research from the streets

Some suggestions in this book come from my own experiences as a single woman. Although I was looking for "the one" by age twenty-seven, I didn't find him until thirty-one and married him at age thirty-three. There were many years of dating jerks, trying to envision a future for myself if I didn't find the right guy, re-evaluating the qualities I wanted in a man, and finding ways to feel truly okay with no guy on the horizon. I learned useful strategies (some in hindsight), which you'll find throughout these pages. I assure you that I'm happily married today with a six-year-old daughter and still use all of the same strategies. Getting clear on your relationship (or any) needs—and figuring out how to make them happen—is ongoing work.

The majority of advice comes from women I interviewed for the documentary *Seeking Happily Ever After*, a feature-length film I made with award-winning producer Kerry David. We were in search of why there are more single thirtysomething women than ever and whether women of all ages are redefining "happily ever after." Is it really married and in a house with a white picket fence before age thirty? Is it the prince coming to rescue a woman on his white horse? Kerry and I talked to several dozen women from around the country and received approximately a hundred e-mails from women of all different ethnicities and backgrounds who wanted to share their stories of being single. What makes our research unique is that we approached our interviews without any agenda or theory to prove. We just wanted to learn what, if any, commonalities single women today shared.

Often we approached women on the street based on the fact that they looked a certain age and wore no wedding band. After they agreed to being filmed, I would pepper them with questions: "What did you think 'happily ever after' looked like as a girl?" "What does it look like today?" "What is the most difficult part of being single?" "What do you love about being single?" I was amazed at how willingly women dropped their guard and told us their most personal and private confessions: "I worry that all my married friends secretly pity me." "I don't know how I'm going to tell my mom that I don't want kids." "I think I'm a better version of myself when I'm not in a relationship."

They also shared their emotional victories, like: "I felt so much better once I finally told my sister to stop pressuring me," and "I finally gave myself permission to stop attending singles events when I realized it depressed me." Some of the advice in this book was culled from their stories about what made interviewees feel better, or worse, about being single. For instance, several women confessed that going home alone for family reunions was the worst, or trying to picture a life unmarried when there were so few attractive models out there. They were too close to the situation to see specific steps they could take to feel better.

Other advice comes from experts ranging from financial analysts, who provide practical steps to feel more secure while you're on your own, to family therapists, who offer successful ways to deal with the pressure and stigma of being unmarried, to singles experts, who have figured out the art of keeping life in balance no matter what one's love life looks like.

On a logistical note, each chapter is filled with personal quotes and anecdotes from women I interviewed. If there is an asterisk by the name, it means that the person requested that I not use her real name or never gave me her real name, or that the story came to me via an unsigned e-mail. In some of the case studies, I switched a few details so the women couldn't be identified, or created a composite of a few different single women who shared similar feelings and experiences.

What stage are you in?

When I organized my interviews with single women into categories, the women fell into one of four stages, which are the structure of this book (each section of the book covering one of the stages). They are:

- **Looking (eagerly) for Mr. Right**, which includes chapters on: (1) looking eagerly for a guy using whatever means available; (2) rebounding after a bad breakup; and (3) dating in a way that doesn't feel like you're on a mission.

- **Experiencing conflicting feelings about being single**, which includes chapters on: (1) dealing with the frustration of waiting for a prince; (2) living life on hold until Mr. Right shows up; and (3) trying to balance commitment and independence when they feel equally essential.
- **Changing love-life goals**, which includes chapters on: (1) experiencing out-of-the-blue fantasies for a traditional wedding; (2) living in a cookie-cutter community when you no longer want that lifestyle; and (3) desiring a wedding/marriage, but only if it fits your unconventional lifestyle.
- **Navigating a marriage-obsessed culture**, which includes chapters on: (1) feeling pressure and frustration around the biological clock; (2) knowing you're not ready for marriage and being judged for it; and (3) finding confidence in your choice to carve out a new path without marriage.

You will likely find that you fall into more than one of these stages, and that you transition into and out of different ones. This book will help you better understand not just where you are now but where you were and where you are heading. The stages don't necessarily happen in a particular order and not all women pass through every one, but one thing's for sure: Single women experience an enormous range of feelings, often conflicting, about their single status. Almost all of the women interviewed—regardless of what stage they're in—feel pressure to get married and feel judged routinely on their relationship behavior. They say that people want to hear the intimate details of their dates and relationships, but nothing about their insecurities, questions, and fears around being single. For that reason, women typically bury their feelings or try to deal with them in isolation. Reading this book, you'll soon see that you're in excellent company and that exploring your feelings is healthy and necessary in finding the right path for yourself.

Time to take action...

This is not a book to read passively. It requires that you sometimes push yourself and occasionally sit in uncertain territory. Stay with it. It takes a concerted effort to figure out what makes you feel good in your love life instead of going along with what everyone expects from you. You will need a journal and a pen so you can do the exercises and answer the questions in each chapter. I strongly suggest doing them, not just thinking about the topic for a couple of minutes and moving on (which I've been guilty of myself). The act of putting pen to paper forces us to be more conscious and adamant about figuring out our real feelings. When we stumble and cross out words and try again, the process helps us work toward the truth and allows us to access our inner voice.

While reading this book, you may find that what you thought you wanted has shifted; it may have even done a full 180 on you. Or perhaps your life goals haven't changed, and you'll find unfamiliar strategies to get to them. Maybe you will discover there is more than one path toward happiness for you. There is no right or wrong goal; there is only what works for you. What matters is learning how to understand and name your needs so you can put steps in place to make them happen. Let's get going.

PART ONE

Looking (Eagerly) for Mr. Right

♥

Yoo-hoo, where are you, Mr. Right?
I'm ready to settle down and maybe
even start a family, but there's one
thing missing—my husband.

1

The Soul Mate Seeker

Definition: You are looking for Mr. Right Now and are doing everything you can to find him.

Pop Quiz

When a friend recommends a brand-new online dating service, do you:

   A   Tune her out while envisioning your upcoming vacation?
   B   Google the service the second you get home?
   C   Restrain yourself from causing her physical damage?

If you answered B, this chapter is for you.

SHARI'S STORY

Thirty-three-year-old Shari said she's been ready to marry and have kids for years. For a while she used online dating services and is now spending heaps of time "putting herself out there," which means going to bars and social activities after work, even if she doesn't feel like it. She signed up for a local volunteer program in hopes of meeting a man while helping the community. Although she's connected with a few guys in the last year, she has not found "the one" and is frustrated.

It's particularly rough when her mother asks, "You're the best woman on the planet. How come so many other women have found men and you haven't?" Shari admits she gets angry and hurt because she is trying her best to find someone and can't explain her single status. "I often wonder," Shari says, "why I have to defend myself when I'm the one who should be cheered up." While Shari appreciates certain things about being single, like enjoying lazy weekends when she feels like it and not having to report to anyone when she stays out late with her friends, she can't help but think of her friends "sharing stories with their husbands over dinner and putting their little ones to bed." Shari adds, "I thought I'd be married with kids at thirty, and I don't even have a boyfriend."

Stage of Singlehood

In your mind, you are doing everything right to try to find your potential mate. You are open to online dating services, blind dates, singles events, and telling practically everyone you know that you're available. Unlike some women, you don't scoff at the notion of comparing dating to a mission; you are a woman of action. The problem is, you're maybe getting tired, possibly even burning out on dating and singles events. It's hard to put yourself out there again and again, and end up empty-handed (empty-hearted) yet again. It's unfair that you are trying so hard and still not meeting anyone. Or maybe you have no problem meeting attractive guys and going on dates—it just never goes anywhere. You think you found the right man, and then he says or does something that makes it so clear he is not, and you're back to square one. Dating or not, you're starting to lose your confidence—wondering if you will ever find your Mr. Right and whether, maybe, there *is* actually something wrong with you.

The Great News

You are clearly an organized, energetic person who knows how to get things done. You couldn't manage your life and juggle all these singles events so well if you weren't. You are open-minded and put achieving your goals before massaging your own ego; after all, you're willing to keep putting yourself out there in spite of not meeting anyone so far. These are good traits. They are even better, more *rewarding* traits, when you can apply this sense of purpose to other parts of your life that haven't gotten enough attention lately. This chapter will help you channel some of your energy and resources back into making you feel good *right now*.

This is also a perfect time to reevaluate and revise what you are looking for in a partner. There is no significant other clouding your judgment with his distracting seductive pheromones; you have the opportunity to start with a blank slate. Plenty of women get so hung up on finding Mr. Right that they forget to think through how they will know whether it's him. Butterflies in your stomach are not enough if you're looking for a long-term partner; nor is it enough to find a guy who wants to spend his life with you (you have to want to spend your life with him too). So what criteria will you use? What traits must the guy have in order for you to commit to him? This is essential planning you can be doing now so you don't waste time on someone who doesn't deserve you.

SHIFT YOUR THINKING

Does your search for a man feel good?

There are some people in your life who insinuate (or tell you blatantly) that your search for Mr. Right is on overdrive. In your head you're just being pragmatic and action-oriented. This was certainly true of Shari from the opening story, and it's true for many women who see dating as a giant numbers game. If you go and go and go, you will find your match—eventually.

Jeannie,* a 44-year-old single woman from Baltimore, said, "I'm not going to be one of those women who sit home in their sweats watching TV and wondering where all the good men have gone. I go out almost every night of the week and will keep doing so until I find the right guy for me." One 27-year-old woman from Memphis said, "Online dating makes me more in control of my dating life. I'll go out with just about anyone unless I can tell he's a real jerk right away. I consider it my job to keep going out night after night to see if I can find my guy."

When I asked these women if they ever get tired from going out so frequently, whether it ever feels like too much, they told me that *of course* it does. Jeannie added, "Dating so much can be a hassle, but you've got to be in it to win it." The single woman from Memphis told me, "It's just going to get harder down the line. I've got to date hard now if I want to meet a guy. I'm not going to get more attractive than this, so it's the time to push."

Hold on. It's one thing to keep the dating doors of opportunity open. It's another to go on an out-and-out manhunt to find Mr. Right. Dating should be pleasurable, at least *possibly* pleasurable. I like how succinctly Rosie Einhorn, LCSW, and Sherry Zimmerman, J.D., M.Sc., put it in their article "Dealing with Dating Burnout" for the Center for Jewish Marriage: "If you feel like you can't go on your next date with a smile on your face or an optimistic attitude, it's time to take a break from dating." It sounds basic, but I think women lose sight of this wisdom sometimes in their drive to find a guy and end the loneliness.

At the very least, it's time to tune in to how you *feel* about spending so much time doing activities with the sole intention of meeting a man. Are you enjoying yourself? Are you getting worn down? How is the rest of your life holding up? Kristine, 30, realized it wasn't just a numbers game, because she was actually becoming a more irritable person from going out on all these online dates that didn't go anywhere. The more she pushed herself to set up new dates, the more let down she felt when things didn't work out. Not only was this surely affecting how she came across on her dates, but it also started making her feel down on herself. "I wondered why I couldn't find anyone, what was wrong with me," she confessed, and that's how she knew it was time to take a break from online dating.

If right now you're realizing that maybe the man mission has gotten a little out of control, the following strategies will help you get your life back on track. It's time to start concentrating on what replenishes you.

ACTION ITEMS

 ### Write it down: What's driving you to find Mr. Right?

Grab your journal and spend five to ten minutes making a list of why exactly you want to find Mr. Right so badly. What are the honest reasons you are longing for a life partner? Don't censor yourself; write down whatever comes to mind. Once you're done, put your pen down, take a deep breath, and look at your list. *Really look at it.* What do you see? Some women I asked realized their answer had less to do with finding "the one" than expected. Below are some responses:

> "I will finally feel normal."
> "I will feel like my real life is beginning."
> "Finally I'll have my mother off my back."
> "I'll be closer to having kids, which is what I want most."
> "I'll get to have the wedding before my grandparent dies."
> "I can stop dating!"

While these women were genuinely looking for love and companionship, it became clear that there were other key reasons they wanted, make that *felt they needed*, to find a husband. Knowing your real reasons—even if you don't like them, even if they embarrass you—will make it possible to see why your life has swung out of balance. It should be stated that there are women who feel plenty good about themselves and simply enjoy the social aspect of singles events and meeting men on a regular basis. This chapter is not for these women; rather it is for any woman who feels a sense of urgency—even desperation—to find a partner. There was Alana, 31, for example, who admitted she is doing everything she can to find a man these days because she "doesn't have that much time before she misses the window of time to have a baby."

For some, this writing exercise will make it clear that you have been looking for a husband in order to prove you're lovable enough ("If a good guy likes me, I'm clearly worthwhile"). Others may find you are so driven because you don't feel entitled to living a full life until you find a husband (chapter 5 will be perfect reading for you). Some of you just want to get Mom (or Grandma or Uncle Fred) off your back because you're sick of all the pressure. Or maybe you have a different reason.

Look back at your notes and see if you can find what you're craving beyond a partner. Is there something you want to prove to yourself or someone else, and what is it exactly? Is there an emotional hole that never got dealt with? Is it a matter of feeling lonely? It might feel scary to put a name to it because that makes the problem seem more real, but it's already real and yanking down your happiness level. There is no question that this issue will keep resurfacing and doing damage if you don't deal with it, so gather your courage and continue on.

Search for answers rather than a man.

Spending less time on the hunt for Mr. Right and more time on feeling good about yourself is the perfect use of your time and energy. In addition to boosting your sense of well-being (what could be more important?), it has the added benefit of making it more likely you will find the right partner. You will be less driven to seek out a man to fix or hide your insecurities, which means you bring your clearest sensibilities into finding someone right for you. Instead of *needing* him, you can approach him from a place of knowing he is lucky to be with you. This is, by the way, extremely attractive to most guys (again, a bonus).

Don't panic if you can't figure out exactly what's creating the urgency to marry. It might take a little time to figure it out. Try talking to a close friend; often it is easier to articulate a problem to someone else and stumble on something illuminating. If you find that you are spinning your wheels, however, consider seeking out a trusted therapist to help. You deserve to feel your best, and paying for a therapist who can help you move forward is the wisest financial investment you'll ever make.

If you are able to pinpoint what has left your confidence waning, explore whether there is a solution you can immediately put into play. For instance, maybe the issue is really that your boss treats you like crap, in which case you make it a priority to try to mend the relationship or start searching the help-wanted ads. Maybe you've been fighting with a toxic friend, and it's time to end that "friendship" once and for all. Can you tell this person your relationship with her is zapping too much of your energy and it's time to part ways? Or maybe you're simply feeling lonely. Why not sign up for a book club or film lecture series that allows you to connect with new people? Sometimes it really is that easy.

It's also possible that you have held on to the belief that Mr. Right will bring happiness for so long that you don't know how to let it go. As one thirtysomething woman told me, "I can't even picture a life without my Mr. Right. It's always on my mind, and I feel like I'm just eternally waiting." Is that true for you? Is it how you want to live? It may also help to talk to friends who say they *have* found Mr. Right about whether that's solved all their problems; you will most assuredly learn the answer is no. Relationships can't cure how you feel about yourself (they can help, but they are not the answer).

You may find that there are also smaller—more straightforward—things you can do to raise your confidence. Women told me they felt better about themselves after "taking a yoga class," "booking a trip somewhere new," "volunteering at a community center," and "taking on a creative project." These kinds of actions may not solve a bigger emotional problem, but they will make you feel stronger while working through it.

Readjust your "wanted" list.

This is also the perfect time to start exploring what you want from a guy—rather than what guys may see in you. Too often women worry about whether a boyfriend is going to be grossed out by their cellulite or turned off by their high salary, instead of asking, What do I want from a man? or What type of guy would be a good partner for me?

Yes, figuring it out may narrow your dating pool, but the guys left in that pool are actually going to be worthy of your time. Rather than investing your nights into casting your net wide and dating all different types of men, put your energy into creating filters so you are more likely to have an enjoyable time on your dates whether they are with Mr. Right or not. Choose three or four qualities your next boyfriend must have—that's plenty, nobody's perfect—and hone in on how you want your guy to treat you. What actions must he take to make him worthy of you? It might be "gives me breathing room," "knows how to cheerlead for me," "isn't stingy"—whatever is right for you. Consider this list of new criteria a contract with yourself—one you'll uphold even if you meet a guy who makes your toes curl but doesn't fit your criteria. It's easy to "forget" your list in the heat of the moment when your brain is screaming "Hot guy at two o'clock!"

If you meet someone who possesses one or two of your essential criteria but lacks another major one, he's out. Not "Possibly, let's give this a little more time"—but O-U-T. Do not back down *now*. Remind yourself that you picked all three criteria because they are *necessary* to your well-being. If one of them is missing from the start, you are walking into a doomed relationship that will, at best, waste your time and, at worst, break your heart. So keep your wits about you and refrain from any kind of flirting with him.

That said, if you meet someone who indeed seems to have the qualities you are looking for, but you're not entirely sure, relax. It's probably too early to tell, which is exactly why you date in the first place. Keep your eyes open and keep checking in to see whether this person meets your needs. If he does, fantastic, keep enjoying this new relationship and see where it goes. If he doesn't, set him loose so you're open to finding the man who is truly right for you.

Step away from the triggers (like Hugh Grant marathons).

If you're the type of gal who can potentially lose a whole weekend watching chick flicks on Lifetime TV, pay attention. Yes, I am talking to those of you who channel-surf upon a rom-com (that's, romantic comedy) starring a fumbling Hugh Grant and must watch it (yet again), and might even cancel previously made plans to do so. "Wait," I can hear some of you pleading, "there's nothing wrong with indulging in these movies! They feed my romantic soul and remind me that my Hugh Grant/Matthew McConaughey/ John Cusack is out there."

Here's the thing: As a smart woman, you know perfectly well these men are *actors* and don't exist in real life. Worse, they genuinely skew the way women think about love. Relationship expert Kimberly Johnson participated in a study at Heriot Watt University in the United Kingdom that examined the influences of romcoms. Her findings: "Films do capture the excitement of new relationships, but they also wrongly suggest that trust and committed love exist from the moment people meet, whereas these are qualities that normally take years to develop." So while you understand logically these movies are fun and frothy fiction, another part of you may be registering these movies as reality, and that's a problem. Basically, you're putting your energy into finding something that doesn't exist.

Tina,* 28, admitted that she would watch romantic comedies over and over when she was sick, and feel better while she was watching, because they were like a dose of supersweet candy. But later that night, after the crash, she would feel depressed about being single and wonder why there wasn't a leading man—say, a funny, cleft-chinned Ryan Reynolds—chasing her through the streets with a bouquet of flowers. As Tina said, "The hours of pleasure I experienced watching love stories did not make up for the sad days to follow where I kept thinking I'm *never* going to have what the lead actress has." Mind you, the lead actress was likely feeling similar sentiments off-camera.

Same thing holds true for spending chunks of time you'll never get back on TLC's *A Wedding Story* or repeats of *The Bachelor* or any other reality TV series where the woman wins the game by scoring an engagement ring. All these shows do is help create the notion that everyone—everyone!—is coupling off and you'd better find someone before you're the only single left.

Also, these shows teach us that love conquers all, and a diamond ring is the answer to all of our problems. Given that this is only true on Planet TV, make the empowering decision to stop buying in and, instead, feed your brain with more inspiring content. Seek out entertainment that makes you feel positive about yourself and advises you on how to bring fun, adventure, and wisdom into your life, rather than a future husband (for suggestions, check out the sidebar "Reading Replacement 101").

Opt out of magazines that equate youth with beauty.

While you're changing the external messages you allow into your life, consider passing on articles that feature fortysomething celebrities who look age nineteen, or that promise to "shed years off your looks." One of the reasons women lose faith in finding their man—and believe time is running out—is that these publications convince us that no one could possibly love us unless we prevent (or, at the very least, eliminate) gray hairs and crow's-feet.

Too many women believe that with each passing year they become less attractive, making it all the harder to potentially meet someone. They'd better put on the speed before things get worse and wrinkles get deeper. Here's how Hannah, a successful (and, it should be noted, beautiful) 25-year-old author, put it: "I hate to admit this, but I feel like even though I am not ready to get married, I am at my peak. I am at my most beautiful, at least that's true according to what society says, and the farther away I get from my peak, the harder it is going to be to find a good husband. I know that sounds terrible, but that's just how it is."

Hannah has a point—or at least she's right about the warping messages we receive about what getting older does to our desirability. On the one hand, young women are advised to avoid rushing into marriage and to spend more time getting to know who they are. This makes sense, as many of the women over age thirty that I spoke with were quick to point out that if they had married boyfriends during their twenties, they'd surely be divorced (or seriously bitter) by now. Hannah herself told me that she was just out of a relationship with an "arrogant" hedge fund guy who was hot but in no way marriage material.

On the other hand, women are hit over the head with the message that what attracts men is beauty and youth. This is hardly news. Anyone who has even once looked at the cover lines of a men's magazine, flipped through *Us Weekly*, or seen women on the big screen age thirty-five-plus knows this to be the case. Women past their early twenties are encouraged to pat expensive night cream under their eyes to avoid sags, keep their bodies in the toned shape of a cheerleader, and consider getting work done (Botox? nip and tuck?).

We are told to want the wisdom, life experience, and resilience that come from maturity, but to retain the smokin' bod of Kim Kardashian. This is how you get Mr. Right. No wonder single women over age twenty-five are often afraid of having their options yanked away. Of course, you might feel pressured to pack in the singles events.

But here's the thing: You can *opt out* of this pressure by refusing to read or listen to content that pushes these ideas. It doesn't even occur to most women that they can consciously avoid it, but that is a real option. Like any bad habit, it takes practice and time, but the payoff is enormous. I know because I've taken the challenge myself, and convinced friends to give it a try.

Krista,* 39, for instance, is a friend who had been studying articles about how to fix her beauty flaws (although I don't see any, mind you) since she turned thirteen. But in the last few years, she decided to stop reading materials that advised losing those last five pounds, plumping her lips, or trying experiments to shave years off her physical appearance. "There were times when I just hated being single so much, I'd look to beauty magazines for tips to help me find a guy faster," she admits, "Following beauty suggestions made me feel like I was being proactive." She said it finally dawned on her, however, that "I don't want to spend one more cent on European creams that reduce fine lines. I want to spend it on things that feed by soul, like a healing arts workshop or a replenishing yoga retreat."

Change the script with your single girlfriends.

Another culprit in making women feel pressured is the conversations they have with close girlfriends, hashing out their dating life. While it feels satisfying to compare war stories (who doesn't love a good vent?), keeping the spotlight on your dating life feeds the idea that happiness rides on finding a partner. Of course, you're going to talk with your girlfriends about finding a man, but it doesn't have to be the first and only thing you chat about. Focus on what you did or saw that week that was interesting or lifted your spirits. If there's not much to draw upon, it is time to try something new: take a Zumba class, sign up for Italian cooking, listen to new music, find a career mentor, become a Big Sister . . . it almost doesn't matter what it is, just try something. Doing new activities helps remind you there is more to life than dating and finding a husband. You'll also see that you can bring joy and balance into your life sans a man, whenever you decide. If you've lost touch with picking an activity for the sole purpose of plea-sure, try activities without any expectations until you land on one you like.

If your single friend is obsessed with finding a man, let her know you've changed your ways. Tell her you're expanding your horizons and trying to focus on other things not testosterone-related. Word of caution: Don't demand she does the same. Hope-fully, she'll be inspired to make changes in her own life, but judging her behavior will probably put a wedge in the friendship. That said, if she stays overly focused on the search—starting and ending every conversation with her latest dating escapade—consider taking a break from her and hanging out with other friends. Fortunately, by adding new activities and adventures, you'll likely make new girlfriends who also share your quest for balance.

Keep your married friends in check.

Maybe what you need is for your married friends to chill out when it comes to your love life. Unfortunately, there are married folk who see your single status as an exciting problem to fix. What starts as an innocent dinner invitation quickly turns into a free-for-all grilling of your love life. In fact, if you don't set limits, married couples can make a sport out of pairing you off. As one single fortysomething claimed, "You would think there is nothing else to talk about in my life other than what guy I'm dating and whether it's going anywhere. I mean, seriously, my romantic life is dull right now, but my married friends still want to hear every brutal detail. Get a life, people!"

You are not a project of the month. Let married friends find a new way to entertain themselves rather than insisting they want to set you up with a great guy they know (and then don't); or playing makeshift therapist by analyzing your dating flaws; or doling out tips on where the good men are. Just about all of the women I spoke with could name at least one married person who was "making them crazy" with all the relationship advice. They just didn't know how to put an end to it.

Tell friends who are treating you like a pet project that you'd like to drop all the attention on your love life. You'll let them know when there is anything to know. Bring up new adventures you plan on taking; ask them about their favorite travels, new restaurants around town, and what TV shows they're watching these days. Hopefully, they'll take the hint and snap out of investigation-mode. For those who won't stop, assume there's something "off" in their own marriage that is leading them to obsess about you. It may be time to take a break from them because you do not need anyone dragging you down; you deserve friends who lift you up. On that note, don't forget to shower with appreciation those friends who support you and reassure you that you're fine as you are.

Schedule the Mom talk: Ask her to stop dwelling on your single status.

Your mother wants you to be happy. She also wants herself to be happy. Both of these, it seems, could be achieved if you would just find a nice guy to settle down with and start making grandchildren for her. In her eyes, it's helpful when she sends you a clipping of a couple that met on eHarmony, asks you about your dating criteria, or tells you (again) about how women today are too picky. To you, it feels like she's saying you have let her down and aren't cutting it. Even worse, she doesn't seem to understand that you are doing everything you can think of to find the right guy, so her comments are even more hurtful.

It's time to end the cycle. First, tell your mom the effects of her "helpful suggestions" and be specific. Ideally, you'll be able to do this in a calm, grown-up voice as opposed to sobs or shrieking (hey, moms have a way of bringing out our inner nutcase sometimes). Start with the belief that her behavior is not malicious, she really is acting this way because she loves you and worries about you. That will change the dynamic of the conversation.

You can say (feel free to riff): "Mom, I know you love me and that you want me to find a man who will love me as well. That's what I want for myself, and I feel sad that it hasn't happened yet. In fact, I'm doing everything I can to put myself out there to find someone. That's why it feels extra hurtful to me when you send me all these suggestions for meeting a guy. It makes me feel pressured and that you're disappointed in me."

She will either apologize on the spot or claim she doesn't know what you're talking about. This is where you take a deep breath and refuse to engage in battle. Instead, explain how you would like her to change. For example, "I'd like it when we're together if you would ask me about work or my friends instead of what I'm doing to find a man." Or, "Instead of sending me wedding announcements, I'd love it if you would send me book or film recommendations." Or, "It would be nice sometimes if you would ask me how I feel about being single rather than trying to fix me up with men."

Give her a little time and space to process this info (and the fact that you really are a grown-up who can take care of yourself). Take accountability yourself by not oversharing personal info with her if you don't want her commentary. If she makes one of her overbearing comments, remind her: "We talked about the fact that I'd like you to stop making comments like this, Mom. Please respect it," and move on. She will come around eventually, when she sees that you are coming from a solid place and mean business.

 ## Tune in to your inner voice: Is your approach to dating *still* working for you?

Keep checking in with your inner voice to see whether dating and singles events feel pleasurable, and schedule breaks when you find yourself thinking, "Ugh, here we go again," or "What's the point?" Dating is *not* just a numbers game; you have to be in a good place emotionally for it to go well. So if you're not getting something positive from it, stop and replenish yourself. As you hone your abilities to take care of yourself and appreciate your own value, the urgency of finding Mr. Right will lift—and you will see what extraordinary company you are to hang out with.

Don't forget to pamper yourself as much as necessary. It's vital when you're doing this kind of self-exploration to go easy on yourself. On your rougher days, make a point of being extra gentle with yourself. Chat with a warm friend on the phone, treat yourself to a comfort-food dinner, book an hour-long massage, or soak in a floral bubble bath. Spoil yourself sometimes for the sake of it; you don't need to wait for a future boyfriend to make you feel worthy of it. Also, remind yourself that while you can't force destiny to put Mr. Right in your path, you are taking active steps to become your strongest self, and this is an amazing accomplishment.

 ## In case of emergency: Write yourself a love note.

For times when you're feeling down, write yourself a letter that describes the things you like about yourself that have nothing to do with your single status. What are you most proud of as far as your achievements and personality? What do you most like about who you are? When you start feeling like something is wrong with you because you haven't found *him*, read this list to remind yourself how much more there is to you than having a husband. Go gangbusters on the flattery. Here's an example:

> *Dear Me,*
>
> *I know you're struggling right now and there are days when you so badly wish you had a partner to share your life with. That is going to happen—really. But until then, this is a reminder to let you know I think you are brave and smart and funny. You are a good friend and always make a point of*

*taking care of those around you who need help. I know
someday you will find someone to spend your life with, but
until then, just remember what a lovely and unique person
you are. Remember to appreciate your wonderful friends
and good life!*

Best, Me

 ## NO NEED TO BANK ON THE PRINCE

One of the hardest challenges for single women who want to
marry is worrying that you won't be able to afford retirement without a partner to help out—and the brutal economy hasn't helped.
A lot of women I know got understandably freaked out in 2008
when they watched their hard-earned 401(k) savings tank along
with the rest of the economy. They desperately wanted to cash
in what was left of their stocks and put the money in a safe money
market account (or hide it in a pillowcase under their mattress).
We were told "bad idea," by experts. If you're still not convinced,
listen to what financial guru Suze Orman has to say: "Sure, a
money market is safe in that its value isn't going to go down. But
when you do that, you put yourself at a much bigger risk: your
money won't grow enough over time to build a big retirement
stash." She goes on to say that a money market account earns
less than 4% right now, and inflation is above 4%; so you are not
building wealth. So don't panic, there is plenty of time for your
funds to grow back—without any royal prince needed.

READING REPLACEMENT 101:
COOL READS THAT *BOOST* YOUR EGO

Why read about looking younger so you can find a man when you could be reading ideas that actually make you feel good? Here's my reading Rx:

- **O, The Oprah Magazine:** In addition to the gorgeous visuals, Lady O's magazine is unique in that it offers women a variety of ways to nourish the soul. It's one of the few women's magazines that seeks to help us fly instead of outing our numerous defects. Plus, the magazine is filled with real-life women who have done big, bold things to inspire us. If they can do it, we can too.

- **Single Minded Women (www.singlemindedwomen.com):** In the interests of full disclosure, I am a regular guest columnist for the "largest online destination for single women," but I chose this pick because it's well-written and gives women plenty of strategies for boosting their career, money, health, and other aspects of their daily lives. Plus, you'll connect with thousands of other single women on days when you feel like the last single woman standing.

- **The Onion (online edition at www.theonion.com):** Part of taking the laser focus off the dating search is remembering to laugh and take yourself a little less seriously sometimes. You won't find inspiring advice here; you will laugh your butt off. With articles like "83-Year-Old Sneaks into 65-to-80 Singles Dance" and "Where Are All These 'Loose Women' My Pastor

(continued)

Keeps Warning Me About?" there's something for everyone who owns a healthy sense of irony and sarcasm.

- **The Savvy Gal (www.TheSavvyGal.com):** A unique online magazine for "motivated, professional women who want more out of life," it offers smart advice "for the real woman in the real world" and does an awesome job of blending written content with short videos that show you exactly how to accomplish specific tasks. Regular columns include "The Money Honey" and "Movers and Shakers."

 ## REMINDER CHECKLIST

1. Write it down: What's driving you to find Mr. Right?
2. Search for answers rather than a man. Determine whether certain things in your life have left your confidence waning, and explore solutions.
3. Readjust your "wanted" list: Choose three or four nonnegotiable items that your next guy must possess.
4. Step away from the triggers. Realize that watching too many romantic comedies is bad for your mental health.
5. Opt out of magazines that equate youth with beauty. Avoid magazine articles that make you feel panicky about running out of time.
6. Change the script with your single girlfriends. Introduce new topics beyond your love life to the conversation.
7. Keep your married friends in check. Don't allow yourself to become their pet project.

8. Schedule the Mom talk: Tell your mother you need her to stop obsessing about the fact that you are still single.

9. Tune in to your inner voice; then make a point of spoiling yourself on occasion instead of waiting for someone else to do it.

10. In case of emergency: Write yourself a mushy love note. It's perfect for times when you need a boost.

2

The Phoenix

Definition: You just got dumped and need helpful ways to rise from the ashes in better shape than ever.

Pop Quiz

You recently suffered an excruciating breakup, and the idea of dating again feels:

- **A** Fine—my ex wasn't right for me anyway.
- **B** Exciting—I get to experience the first kiss again!
- **C** Horrifying—I can't believe I have to start glammin' it up on first dates again.

If you answered C, this chapter is for you.

MEREDITH'S STORY

Meredith,* 27, spent the last four years of her life devoted to her boyfriend Todd, and was certain they'd marry. Friends and relatives on both sides joked around easily with them about the future wedding and babies. They'd even looked at engagement rings once.

"It was all mapped out," Meredith said. That is, until one night over dinner, Todd explained to Meredith that he was breaking up with her because he just "couldn't handle the fact that his life was spelled out." Meredith was furious, "as in I couldn't see straight for days." But that anger was far better than the despair that came afterward. "The worst moment for me was when I finally changed my Facebook relationship status from 'in a relationship' to 'single.' It just made the whole thing so public and real," Meredith said. She quickly added that she knew she'd better "rebound quickly" because she didn't want to "miss the good window of meeting someone."

Stage of Singlehood

You thought you found your soul mate. You would have sworn that the search was over and dating was ancient history. Maybe your friends and family even confirmed that you two were the perfect match, and it was assumed you'd grow old together. You planned on growing scrapbooks full of vacation shots, dreaming of retirement together, and entwining your lives. No more first dates, no more awkward getting-to-know-you conversations, no more wondering when the *one* will show up. Then *poof!* he dumped you. In addition to the heartache and severe ego-stomping, you have to deal with the pragmatics of separating your personal stuff, divvying up items, and basically yanking apart your lives. How did this happen?! The idea of starting from scratch makes you depressed, maybe even infuriated. How many times can you go through this before throwing in the towel?

The Great News

Remember back in grade school when you played kickball or hop-scotch and got a "do over" because of some fluke? It was great because you got another shot at doing things right. Well, once you recover from the heartache (or, possibly, full-on meltdown) of this past breakup, you'll realize that you just got yourself a relationship do-over. Too many women end up marrying the wrong guy because it seems less stressful than starting the search all over again. But life is too short—and you are too worthwhile—to settle with the wrong someone.

Also, you are not starting from scratch the next time you date, even if it feels that way at this moment. You now have a better understanding of what works and doesn't work for you in a relationship, and what red flags to look for. If you don't have a handle on this, no worries, because this chapter is devoted to making sure you will. Trust me: while you may be shedding tears into a half-eaten pint of Rocky Road and bemoaning your loss, you are going to be ever so thankful that this breakup gave you the opportunity to figure out how to make yourself stronger and find a much better match.

SHIFT YOUR THINKING

Sadness is not the enemy.

Well-meaning folks will tempt you to forgo grieving by encouraging you to dive back into the dating pool. Some will write down the name and phone number of a "perfect" single man they know and tell you to call before he's off the market. Others will tell stories about how their first cousin joined an online dating service after her breakup and met the man of her dreams within a month. Some will suggest you avoid spending even one minute being sad, because there are plenty of single men still available and your ex doesn't deserve one iota of thought. The basic messages are "Stop dwelling" and "There are plenty of fish in the sea, so cheer up."

These people are idiots.

Let me try that again. These people are misguided. They believe that sadness and grief should be avoided because why suffer if you can feel good? What's the point? The point is that what you're going through is a big deal. As grief therapist, Dr. Maurice Turmel, Ph.D., put it on his website (www.howtocopewithgrief andloss.com), a breakup is "the death of possibilities, a future full of promise and plans that were evolved during your better days together." He goes on to say that experiencing loss, sadness, and grief are normal, and it is appropriate to "go through a period of mourning and bereavement over the death of possibilities." Basically, what you're experiencing is painful, and you need to honor that by moving through the pain and not trying to outrun it. In fact, you can make things much worse by denying your grief. Experts at BUPA, an international health care company in the UK, state that for those who don't deal with their feelings, "grief can carry on for longer than normal, or never become resolved. You may find it hard to acknowledge the bereavement at all or you may remain numb, or find it impossible to get past the mourning stage."

If you're willing to go through the grieving now—and face your own accountability—you can stack the odds of finding a terrific guy the next time around. This chapter will help you figure out why you're drawn to certain types of men, whether you are making healthy choices, and how you can adjust what type of man you're drawn to. So while this may mean you have to invest temporarily in extrastrength tissues and economy-size Visine, grieving now and challenging old assumptions is the way to take care of yourself and set things right. This far beats choosing the wrong guy over and over. As the saying goes, "Insanity is doing the same thing over and over and expecting a different result." So, on to recovery.

ACTION ITEMS

Commit to two to three months of no dating.

You heard me: if you are just out of a serious, committed relationship, *no dating* for at least a couple of months—two if you thought he might be the one, three if you were sure he was. "Of course, I wouldn't date," you may be thinking, "the very idea is absurd." But for a lot of women it's easy after the initial shock wears off to jump back on the dating bandwagon as a distraction from grief. It's much more fun to be shopping for your next potential guy than wallowing and stewing.

Jae, 33, told me that she signed up on Match.com a couple days after breaking up with her boyfriend. "I'm not ready to date," she claimed. "I just wanted to assure myself that there are good guys left on the market."

When I asked her if she contacted anyone, she said, "Well, only one guy. He was really compatible with me and sometimes you have to just go for it even if the timing is not great, right?"

Not right! This guy didn't respond to Jae's email, leaving her depressed and much more worried about getting back into the dating world. Even if he did write back and suggest a date, the timing most likely would have wrecked any potential between the two. *No dating.* Again, the goal is to move through your grief—no matter how uncomfortable it is—so that you can leave it behind and start making better choices for yourself.

Go ahead and release the "ugly cry."

Priya, 39, who blogs about her single life on Indi-chick (www .indi-chick.blogspot.com), had this to say of her recent breakup: "I truly thought that my long wait was over. I just clicked with him—and for the first time in my life I legitimately believed that all this time I really had been waiting for him, for lack of better words, I had been waiting for my Last Best Hope." She added, "It's the kind of thing that makes you want to fling everything off the top of the desk you're typing on and lay down on it, beating your fists and feet and sobbing your eyes out and crying so hard that your eyes hurt and you may even drool a time or two before it's all over."

All women should give themselves time to bawl their eyes out. This may be a week for some, and two weeks for others. Basically, take as long as you need without letting it become your new lifestyle. As Dr. Marvin H. Berman said in his article "The Grieving Body: Learning to Let Go and Live Life": "There needs to be time and space given to the experience of grieving and loss in the service of healing and recovery. You need to create space to cry and feel whatever is present in the moment emotionally and find ways to express those feelings with your body." He suggests crying, screaming, hitting the bed with a tennis racquet or your hands, kicking the bed, twisting a towel, and/or tearing up old phone books (well, if you've got the rage, tear the page).

If you're having trouble getting tears to flow, listen to gut-wrenching music (for me, Kate Bush's song "This Woman's Work" takes me down in less than five notes), watch sentimental films like *My Sister's Keeper* and *The Joy Luck Club*, think about all the things you're going to miss about your ex, cry over the frustration of having to start dating all over again. Go on a short-term hiatus from friends who insist you get your act together. At this moment you do not have to pull together (you just have to make sure you feed and water yourself and avoid getting fired). Remember: If you don't feel the feelings now, your grief is just going to come back to bite you in the ass at a worse time, like, say, a couple months into finding a worthwhile guy you hoped to make a life with. It could go something like this: Your new guy will ask you whether you want to go out for sushi, and you'll burst into tears while recalling the last time you ever shared a California roll with your ex. Or you will be on a first date with a fantastic guy who you won't even give a chance to because you're already anxious that he might dump you and break your heart all over again. So grieve now until there are no new tears left to cry. Only then is it time for the next step.

Get rid of all traces of him.

I'm not suggesting a crime with a body bag, tempting as that might be. Get rid of his stuff. All of it—the Pop-Tarts he kept in your cabinets, the so-soft old T-shirt that he left on your floor, the pillowcase that smells like his aftershave. You're not doing yourself any healing favors by keeping his belongings on display. Return valuables to your ex if that feels right; donate the rest to Goodwill—it's a good deed and a tax write-off too (if you need inspiring music to keep your energy up, see the sidebar "Kick-Ass Songs to Play While Packing Your Ex's Stuff"). Go it alone if you like; or ask a friend to come over with garbage bags and/or plan a reward for getting through this—a martini night out with the girls, buying a new favorite candle for your transformed space, or enjoying a matinee film escape. Too often, in dealing with breakups, women hold on to their ex's stuff and see getting rid of it as the *final* step. But to do the challenging mental exploration that comes next, it's essential to be working in a clean space.

This also means keeping the flesh-and-blood him out of your domain. No phone calls (drunk dialing or sober), no one-last-hurrah sex, no pretending you can be friends because you are mature adults and can handle it. Even if you do want to be friends at some point, the only way it's going to happen is to first take a long break (as in, a year-long break). Do not return his e-mails checking up on you or his phone messages saying he misses you and made a mistake. If you know in your heart this is over, cut the ties and make it easier on both of you. Somebody has to be the grown-up here. It may as well be you.

Perhaps most challenging of all, get rid of the "virtual" him. By that I mean it's time to sever your connections to him on all social networking sites, whether it's LinkedIn, Facebook, MySpace, whatever. If you're thinking, "No, no, I can handle it; it's not a big deal," you are deluding yourself. You know as well as I do that you are checking his status report for clues, trying to figure out whether he's moved on or not. Is he dating? Has he changed his relationship status and identified himself as single? You say, "I'll just peek at his profile, it won't hurt," and then *wham!* there's a picture of him captioned "What happens in Vegas stays in Vegas." Or his Facebook status says, "Way too old for strip poker . . ." and you're livid. It feels like he's cheating on you; only he's not because you've already broken up. Not only is this something you can't handle, it's something you shouldn't *have* to handle. Do the big-girl thing; de-friend him.

 ## Write it down: What do your exes have in common?

Make a list in your journal of what drew you to your exes and what, in retrospect, you ended up disliking about them. Be specific. This may take you five minutes—it may take you twenty. Don't worry about the time spent; just make sure you have a thorough list.

Okay, you're still banned from dating, in spite of the fact that many women often get itchy about now to find a replacement guy. It's hard because you want to comfort yourself, having been through such a painful time—and a hot guy who makes you laugh seems the height of comfort. The problem is that if you go back to dating now, you're going to end up with the same type of guy who won't work out for similar reasons as the last guy, and you will end up back here again. So forgo the announcement that you're back on the dating market. It's time to redefine what makes a guy attractive.

There is a good chance you'll end up seeing certain patterns on your list, and this is helpful—so don't freak out if you see you've basically been dating the same type of loser your whole life. Your selection of guys may share physical traits, such as body build, eye color, or height. Likely you'll also see that your men share certain personality traits, for good and bad. Are you drawn to the laid-back guy who never shows up on time? Or the wise-ass that needs to be "on" all the time? When I was single, I kept picking tall, funny, creative artists who were moody and needed emotional support. It took me about ten years—and major soul-searching—to break that nasty habit.

Next, circle all of the negative traits your exes have in common and—here comes the hard part—see if you can figure out *why* you're drawn to this type. Is there someone you know (your father? a sibling? a childhood crush? a mentor? an enemy?) who shared these same traits? It's not enough to know what your pattern is, you've got to figure out *why* you've created this pattern in the first place, understand why it doesn't work for you, and then develop new criteria for a partner. Once you do this, you're already on your way to finding a fantastic partner.

If you come up blank, sit with these questions for a few weeks and see if something shifts. You may have an illuminating dream, or the answer may come when you're not thinking about it. If you still can't get to why you're drawn to the men of your past, however, consider asking close friends for their take on the situation, especially if they have known you for a long time and met your exes. Or talk to your mom if she's tuned in to your life and you trust her opinion. If none of this works—and you aren't able to figure out why you make the bad choices you do—it's time to meet with a trusted therapist.

Carol Ann,* single at 41, said, "I chose guys for years who were thrill seekers. If a guy had a motorcycle or knew how to ski black-diamond trails, I would drool for him. Eventually I realized that these guys might have fascinating stories, but they were terrible partners because they got bored easily in a stable relationship." She says that once she realized this, she decided she had to change her criteria because she really wanted a man who wouldn't get antsy in a healthy ongoing relationship and leave every few months for his dose of adrenaline. "I had to purposefully change my type to nicer guys with just a touch of thrill seeker," she said. "This meant being extra in tune for the first six months or so, making sure to stay away from high-octane guys, but it got easier to recognize them and walk away."

Denise, 39, was picking really sweet guys who adored her but who didn't have ambition, which became a major problem for her. "It has nothing do with financial success for me," she said, "it's about finding guys who have drive and believe in themselves. I finally realized that was something I needed in my life to be happy, and in others as well."

Hold on to your notes and ideas about old types because they will guide you in your future choices. If you see during your date that your new interest shares the old fatal flaw, see it for the red flag that it is rather than making excuses for it or defending it. It's easy in these moments to think, "Well, I don't want to be too picky," or "This could be my last chance at love, so I'll make an exception." No! You already know that making major exceptions leads you to the wrong guy. No matter how adorable/sexy/fantastic new-guy-on-the-block is, he is not for *you*, so end things quickly. You'll feel bad about it for one night (maybe two), and then you're going to dance a jig around your living room once you realize that you just spared yourself months of inevitable heartache. It takes work to get to this place, but it will get easier. You will get faster at spotting the red flags, and closer to finding a partner that you deserve.

It may also take you a little while to appreciate good men who don't fit your old type. After all, you're dealing with a serious habit. Think of it like comfort food. You've been reaching for the same bag of salty chips in your kitchen for months and maybe years because it always tastes delicious and comforting. Opting to swap these chips for a healthier comfort food may feel weird. It will look and taste different, and it may take a bit for you to appreciate the long-term benefits (like a boost in your energy levels). Same thing holds true for choosing a healthier guy: you are going to have to open your mind (and libido) to a new type and allow yourself enough time to experience the potential benefits.

After breaking up with my last funny boyfriend before meeting my husband, I realized I was sick of taking care of guys with enormous mood swings and tantrums. I made a conscious point of choosing men online who had a sense of humor but weren't notably sarcastic, who seemed steady and relatively un-needy. "Generous" became a quality I searched for. I dated about ten different guys over the course of a year. While I didn't feel immediate chemistry with most of these guys, I dated a few of them several times and let myself get used to being with nice, stable guys. By the time I met my husband online (No. 11), I was not only attracted to him right away, but I was also ready to commit to a good guy. I'd broken my old habit and never looked back. My old "type," which seemed so sexy at the time, now seems self-absorbed and life-sucking.

 ## Tune in to your inner voice: Is there an emotional hole to fill?

Sit in a quiet place, close your eyes, and ask yourself: "Is there some specific trait that the guys I'm attracted to bring and that is missing in my own life?" This is always a tough question, but if you can name what's missing, you can create it for yourself or find it in people other than your boyfriends. Spend several minutes being quiet and seeing what comes back from your inner voice.

If you, like Carol Ann, love thrill-seeking guys, maybe you need more endorphin rushes in your life and it's time to figure out how to provide your own "rushes." If you have a thing for snarky guys that can border on rude, hang out with a guy at the office who has this trait. Stop seeking it in a potential partner because a guy who makes snarky jokes at the expense of others is going to eventually turn his vicious tongue on you. If you love dating men who have different values from you because you're curious about people, get involved in local politics or take an exploratory vacation that taps into this curiosity. Partners who have values that clash with yours are intriguing for a few months—until the hormones wear off and you're left exhausted from fighting.

Meghan,* 26, went through this kind of exploration and was surprised at what she learned. "When I looked at what attracted me to my exes, I realized that they all had the silliness and spontaneity that was missing from my own childhood. It made so much sense that I would be drawn to them," she said. "There wasn't only one reason why these relationships led to breakups, but I do think that I put so much focus on the lighthearted quality that I didn't pay attention to big flaws they had." Meghan said that the next step for her was to take off a couple of months from dating and figure out ways to bring spontaneity into her own life so she wouldn't depend on that from men anymore. "Instead of looking to a boyfriend to come up with some cool dating ideas, like bungee jumping or a sushi-making class, I pushed myself to plan these events," Meghan said. "I took friends or went alone. It was weird at first, but then it was wonderful. Thank God I did this because now I can focus on other things I want from a man, like making sure he is centered and has goals for himself."

Speaking of which, for those thinking, "I can't help who I am attracted to, it's chemistry," that is a lie you tell yourself. Okay, yes, we can't help that we respond in a certain way to specific physical attributes and pheromones. We can blame biology for that, as well as for the way we respond to "love chemicals" in our brain, like dopamine and serotonin, which researchers including anthropologist Helen Fisher say influence our choices. But— and this is a big but—we can retrain our brains to find certain qualities attractive. After three years of interviewing single women, I am certain of that. The best part of being single past your mid-twenties is that you know you are no longer a slave to your hormones. You can tap into intuition, wisdom, and experience. At some point, for instance, many of us stop being attracted to the "bad boy" who treats us like garbage, usually after, oh, the fifth or so time we end up getting our heart stomped on. We start out seeing bad boys as rebellious and adventurous, but eventually see them for the immature brats they are. Hormones be damned.

While you're striving to be more careful about men you select, you may be overly sensitive and worried about picking the right type. You may see more red flags than you *should*, and even start making them up when they're not there. This is just you going from one extreme to another, and with practice you are going to find a middle ground and learn you can trust your instincts.

Write it down: What misbehavior can you own up to?

Okay, you now know the fatal flaw(s) in your relationships. The next step is to examine your own accountability—beyond your selection process. This book is not about blaming you. But to be truly fulfilled, on your own or in a relationship, you need to be able to take responsibility for your own actions. This does not mean beating yourself up for what you've done wrong; it's about figuring out how to make better choices that help you feel grounded.

Grab your pen again and write down whatever faulty behavior exes have accused you of more than once. Get real, here; you don't have to show it to anyone. When you look at the list (even if it's a list of one item), how do you feel? Does your gut tell you that this behavior *is* actually a problem that's getting in your way? If so, start examining where the behavior comes from and what you can do to change it. If you're consistently accused of showing up late or being bossy, for instance, this is the exact right time to nip the problem in the bud.

Again, if you can't think of any flaws, call your closest girlfriend and ask her if she sees noteworthy patterns, because you're trying to do things differently. Warning: Do *not* bite her head off when she gives you an answer! Just listen, and no matter what she brings up, tell her you're going to think about that.

Jill,* 35, admits that she relied on a friend to help her figure out why her relationships kept leading to breakups. She says she tried to figure it out on her own but just kept getting stuck, so she eventually called a friend from childhood and asked for feedback. Her friend told her that, in truth, Jill can be really guarded in her relationships with men and doesn't seem to give them the benefit of the doubt.

"It sucked hearing that," Jill says, "and my first response was to deny it and blame the guys. But I thought about it a lot and realized that it was true. Undoubtedly, it was because my father left the family when I was a girl and I spent my whole childhood listening to mom railing against men, about how they are pigs and they cheat. My mom got over it and even remarried, but I had a hard time replacing those old messages. So I'd start a relationship with a guy I really liked and I would expect him to cheat. I don't think any of them cheated, but they did leave, and I can see now that all my accusations and suspicions were a big part of it."

Jill said that she tried dating with a more open mind once she realized this, but her old habits were dying way too hard. So she found a therapist who was able to help her go back and explore old family dynamics and the effect her dad's abandonment had on her. "It was about a year trudging through this old crap until I felt ready to date again," she said. "It was awful going through it and reliving some of it again, but I am so happy I did because I feel so much freer now, like a twenty-pound pack of resentment was removed from me."

Martyrdom is unnecessary; add heaps of pleasure.

Just because you're doing soulful work right now does not mean you have to hole up and think about this stuff 24/7. I'd advise you don't. You're going to need breaks from deep thinking, and pleasant breaks at that. Sit by the window and feel the sun streaming in. Make sure you're taking full, deep breaths if you get a little stressed. Luxuriate in a bubble bath with lavender bath beads. Listen to soothing classical music.

Beyond just relaxing, make a point of going out to have fun. Make a list of things you've always wanted to try, anything from "Take a tour bus ride of my own city" to "Try out the new caramel-flavored latte at the local bakery." Add something upbeat to each day, which you deserve and, by the way, you don't move through grief any faster by withholding pleasure from your life. Take a nature walk during your lunch break; rent a tried-and-true movie that lifts your spirits; call an old friend that you haven't spoken with in a while.

I also recommend volunteering somewhere once a week to get out of your own head. If you're thinking, "Nah, I don't have the energy," you'll be surprised by how much energy you'll find after helping others for an afternoon. Whether it's reading to the blind, mentoring a child, handing out food to the homeless, or working with abandoned pets, you'll leave feeling charged by giving back to the world—and it's likely you're going to end up with some perspective on your own amount of suffering. Try VolunteerMatch.org or 1-800-volunteer.org to find ideas in your area.

Call for backup.

Then there's the matter of the outside world, and how others will deal with this breakup. Hopefully, you've got an awesome friend(s) who knows how to cheerlead for you as you work through the internal exploring and also keeps an eye on you to make sure that you're not holing up in your oversize sweats for too long. Let this friend help you find your independent footing again; you both know you'll get her back next time.

If you don't have close friends (maybe, unfortunately, you put most of your emotional energy into your ex), call some casual friends or acquaintances and ask them out for coffee. Do not dump your problems on them when you get together; instead start building relationships with them by getting to know them better. It will feel good to build a circle of people you can trust and who you care about. (Just a reminder: When you find your next guy, make sure you continue to make time for these new friends; they are not just there to boost you up until you find your next guy.)

Shut down the pity party.

Then there are those who succeed in making you feel worse than ever. Maybe it's the uncle who says, "It feels like every time I take a breath you're breaking up again." Or the less-than-stellar friend who announces, "God, I can't believe you guys broke up, he was so great!" Or the sister who says, "There are going to be no men left for you if you keep plowing through them." Or the boss who offers endearing suggestions like, "I heard you broke up. I hope your work isn't going to suffer."

That said, if you're like many women, there's nothing worse and more distracting than people looking at you with furrowed brow, tsk-tsking about your hardship, as if your home blew away in a tornado. What's crucial here is that you *not* get sucked into these lame observations or enter the pity party. You are doing too much work to get to a better, stronger place and you need to keep your focus there.

Here's the thing about pity. If you're not in a good place emotionally, it can be undoing. I like the following description of pity, which a woman living with a genetic disorder wrote on her blog, Brilliant Mind Broken Body (www.brilliantmindbroken body.wordpress.com): "When someone is pitied, they stop being a human being to the person who is pitying them. Instead, they are a thing—an object. We become a disability, a problem, a sad story." She goes on to say that pity "sets us apart." I am obviously not comparing the scope of living with a genetic disorder to breaking up with a loved one, but I think the writer is exactly right when she suggests that nobody wants to become an object—in this case, the "thing that can't hold on to a man."

The good news is that it's hard for anyone to effectively pity you if you don't feel bad for yourself. If you go home to a family event looking and sounding ashamed because you're solo, then you are going to draw pity, no question. If, on the other hand, you come to a peaceful place about being single (remembering that you could be married to some jerk if all you wanted was to get married), pity will deflect off you.

Remind yourself that these folks doling out the "Poor you" and "It must be so hard" commentary need to tell themselves this because it makes them feel better about their own life, or because they have bought into the old-fashioned ideas of how women's lives *should* look. Why waste your time trying to justify or defend being single to them? Don't bother. Instead, in a neutral tone tell them, "I appreciate your concern, but I'm doing well," or redirect them with "Thanks, I'm fine. How's that project you're working on?" If they don't get the hint, get out of the line of fire. Smile, excuse yourself, and exit stage left.

Schedule the Mom talk: Ask her to stop referring to your ex as "the one that got away."

Perhaps your mother was secretly planning a wedding guest-list, positive that your ex-boyfriend was the one. She was excited about the idea of knowing that you were settling down, and now she's irritated that her dream is over. Her way of letting you know is either indirect ("Do you remember how Rob used to tell the funniest jokes?") or direct ("I don't understand why you let someone as wonderful as Rob go!"). What's not going to help is trying to convince your mom that your ex was not the one and yelling at her for taking sides.

Instead, tell her directly that your relationship with your ex-boyfriend is over. You can tell her that you're sorry she's disappointed but that you have moved on and now she needs to as well. You would like her to stop mentioning your ex. Depending on how it's going, you can tell her that you are going to be experimenting with dating new types that you think will be healthier for you. You'd love it if she could be supportive; if she can't, you will have to quit sharing.

If she still won't let go (you'll know because she will insist you should try to patch things up with your ex), ask her why, exactly, she is so upset about your breakup. It might be that she is worried about you being able to take care of yourself, in which case you can hopefully assure her that you're doing just fine and don't need a man to take care of you. It might be that she wished she married a man like your ex. Who knows? Don't get caught up in defending yourself to your mother; you are just trying to better understand her. Remember, these are *her* anxieties, not yours.

Ultimately you may have to just agree to disagree about whether your ex was the right one for you—and insist she drop it.

Now get back in the game.

At this point, you've determined what's gone wrong in past relationships, including your own accountability, and come up with a plan for selecting a new type. You've found friends to cheer you on, and ways to cheer *yourself* on. You can see yourself for all that you are—way more than just a woman who's single—and appreciate your finer qualities. Sure you'd like to find a fantastic guy to share your life with, but you're not going to pick just anyone who makes your heart race. You're no longer looking for a *potential* partner ("he could be the one if I work with him a little"). A guy either fits your criteria or he doesn't. If it's the latter, you're not wasting your time, even if he shares a somewhat uncanny resemblance to George Clooney. Now you are ready to get back in the dating pool.

 ## In case of emergency: Remove the "ex" from "text."

You've been doing great, concentrating on healing and moving on. Just when you're certain you're totally over him, you have a weak moment. One night, one stupid cocktail! Suddenly you just need to hear his voice. Do *not* drunken speed-dial or text your ex. You think, "I just want to say a quick hi," and "I'm sure I'll get his voice mail and hang up." But then he surprises you by answering, and suddenly you are awash in missing him. "Um, hey, it's me . . ." you say and then can't think of anything else. There *is* nothing else. He's either going to invite you over for a booty call or tell you he's seeing someone. This is a lose-lose with an added kick to your dignity. Skip the drama and dial a friend who can remind you of what you couldn't stand about him. Jot down the list so you can do this for yourself next time. Now for the brave part: Delete his phone number once and for all. There is no good reason to keep it stored.

 SAVINGS FOR ONE, PLEASE

Part of the breakup headache right now might be that you were counting on having a partner who would help burden some financial costs. Maybe you were going to get a place together, which would have been affordable for two. Or, you were borrowing certain things of his—a car, computer, iPhone—because it was easy enough and meant you didn't have to shell out a lot of cash. Now that you're back to solo status, you want to come up with a sound financial plan that makes you feel confident and steady currently—and in the future, regardless of meeting a new guy. Assess your financial situation, being completely honest about any debt or loans that have to get paid back. This is not the time to gloss over items. When you see this list, do you feel relatively confident about making it on your own? If not, hire a financial adviser to help you.

KICK-ASS SONGS TO PLAY WHILE PACKING YOUR EX'S STUFF

These songs are so damn empowering, you're going to want to break up with him all over again.

1. "Strong Enough" by Cher; favorite line: *"I am strong enough to know that you've got to go!"*
2. "Before He Cheats" by Carrie Underwood; favorite line: *"The next time that he cheats, oh, you know it won't be on me."*
3. "Single Ladies (Put a Ring on It)" by Beyoncé Knowles; favorite line: *"If you like it, then you should have put a ring on it!"*
4. "Leave (Get Out)" by JoJo; favorite line: *"Tell me why you looking so confused when I'm the one that didn't know the truth."*
5. "Live Your Life" by T.I. featuring Rihanna; favorite line: *"Stop looking at what you ain't got and start bein' thankful for what you got."*
6. "Not Gon' Cry" by Mary J. Blige; favorite line: *"Swallowed my fears, stood by your side, I shoulda left your ass a thousand times."*
7. "Since You Been Gone" by Kelly Clarkson; favorite line: *"You had your chance, you blew it. Out of sight, out of mind."*

And, of course, the cliché and yet all-time best breakup song of all time . . .

8. "I Will Survive" by Gloria Gaynor; favorite line: *"I'm not that chained up little person still in love with you!"*

☑ REMINDER CHECKLIST

1. Commit to two to three months of no dating. This is a time to devote to making healthy choices around your love life.

2. Go ahead and release the "ugly cry." It's best to feel your sadness at high intensity now so you can put it behind you.

3. Get rid of all traces of him. Don't leave reminder items of him around your place.

4. Write it down: What do your exes have in common?

5. Tune in to your inner voice. It's time to find out if there is some hole in your life that you can fill without a boyfriend.

6. Write it down: What kind of misbehavior can you own up to?

7. Martyrdom is unnecessary; add heaps of pleasure. Give yourself plenty of rewards and indulgences for doing this emotional heavy lifting.

8. Call for backup. Time to bring in your friends for support and to help with the healing process.

9. Shut down the pity party. Do not let others turn your short-term misfortune into a tragedy.

10. Schedule the Mom talk. Tell your mother she needs to stop referring to your ex as the "one who got away."

11. Now get back in the game. You're officially ready to start dating whenever you like.

3

The Organic

Definition: You prefer to leave your love life up to destiny rather than hunting for men in a calculated way.

Pop Quiz

The idea of spending an evening speed dating is:

A Demoralizing. You'd rather risk becoming a spinster living with a house full of cats.

B Possibly okay. The worst that happens is you leave with a hilarious story.

C Fantastic. Hey, it's all about boosting your odds, right?

If you answered A, this chapter is for you.

JANE'S STORY

Jane,* 41, confesses that her dating life right now is "pretty non-existent." Although she goes out all the time, it's usually with couples and she's the only single person. Why isn't she dating much? For one thing, she wants to meet a guy "the old-fashioned way, in a bookstore or at a park," not by attending singles events. The idea of getting together with friends and going to a bar for the explicit purpose of meeting men gives her the creeps, so it's harder to find someone. But if it takes her longer to find someone, so be it, she says.

Still, Jane recognizes that there are costs for doing it this way: "In between dates, months can go by and I start to miss sex a lot. I also miss falling asleep in someone's arms and waking up there. I love that feeling of connection." She feels pressure from family members and often worries that her eggs are drying up. But, according to Jane, she would rather put up with these hardships than make her whole life about finding a man and feeling like she is "on a hunt." If only she could get everyone else in her life to understand.

Stage of Singlehood

Enough with everyone telling you to get more assertive about finding a man. It's just not *you*. Maybe you can't stand the idea of feeling like an aggressor on the prowl; maybe you're burnt out from your prior efforts to find Mr. Right. What you want now is to find your man naturally—you spot each other across the room, smile, and approach each other. Maybe it's at a bookstore, local café, lecture, or concert . . . just as long as it's not a planned singles event. You prefer to find love with a little mystery and intrigue. When did courtship die anyway? And why does everyone see your approach to dating as a cop-out?

The Great News

You know what works for you—in this case, refusing to get caught up in an aggressive dating approach at the expense of the rest of your life. This means you aren't going to suffer the torment of meeting a guy you contacted online whose picture was taken ten years ago (when he had more than three strands of hair). Nor are you going to waste a precious evening on a depressing singles event where the women are infinitely cooler than the men.

Also, in sticking to your own approach, you will become more practiced at staying true to yourself, and deflecting outside pressure. It takes courage to follow your own path, as you well know, when everyone and her mother is claiming you would be so much happier if you would just put yourself out there. You realize *you're* the only one who knows what is right for you, which puts you light-years beyond most people, single or hitched. This is all great news, so long as you make sure your reasons for going about the search in your own way comes from a strong, grounded place and not from fear, anxiety, or trying to prove a point. This chapter will help you figure that out, and then get you back on track if necessary.

SHIFT YOUR THINKING

Does your decision come from the right place?

You have made the decision to avoid the chaos of speed dating, online dating sites, professional matchmakers, and theme nights like "Find your match blindfolded!" at the local bar. You can't help but feel these activities are forced, awkward—and desperate. Maybe this comes from your romantic belief that you and Mr. Right will bump into each other due to destiny. Maybe it comes from attending singles events in the past, and recalling how depressed and demoralized you felt afterward. You vowed to stop wasting your time and money.

That was certainly the case for several women I interviewed. Karen, 33, said: "I'm no longer on a manhunt like I was in my twenties. I now feel like, if it's going to happen, it's going to happen." Fabienne, 35, stated: "I'm no longer willing to go to a bar to meet men. Those men are there, I believe, for one particular purpose, and that purpose doesn't serve me." Whatever your reason, you have made the call that you're going to find your next guy the traditional way, and the more people who get on your back to "get out there," the more you will dig in your heels and stay committed to your plan.

If this is a decision that continues to feel right and true, carry on. But if you feel yourself becoming rigid in your rules and overly set in your dating ways, ask yourself: Would you allow yourself to change your mind and try a more unconventional dating option if the mood struck? Are you so insistent on persuading everyone you're just fine that you are keeping part of yourself closed off? Are you allowing yourself to experience the (normal) mixed feelings about being single? Do your decisions come from a place of confidence or a fear of rejection? Not sure? Keep reading.

ACTION STEPS

Know if you're self-aware—or scared.

It's easy to be resolute about your choice to seek love the old-fashioned way given that you're constantly put on the defensive ("Why don't you just *try* singles night at the local pub?" "You're never going to find someone if you're not willing to take risks!"). If you show even the tiniest amount of wavering, others might jump on the bandwagon and ratchet up the pressure. If your commitment to your approach comes simply from knowing what works best for you, then that's grand.

If, on the other hand, you are partially avoiding today's dating options because you are afraid of being hurt, that's another issue. Putting yourself online or in a room full of strangers means others will be judging you (that's the nature of these events). In fact, *many* men will be judging you just as you'd judge them. Is *this* the part that upsets you? Why? Because if you're refraining from these options because of low confidence levels and fear of being rejected, it's important to figure out what's making you feel *less than*. The major priority here needs to be working on that issue so you can nourish your self-worth and make decisions from a place of strength. If you're not able to work through your lack of confidence on your own, find a reputable therapist in your area who can help you. This obstacle is not something to hope will go away or get fixed when you find Mr. Right; it is something to take care of now and on your own so you are able to make healthy choices and feel good moving forward.

If you choose to pass on modern dating strategies and opt for destiny's arrival, it may take longer to find someone (that's not a given but a definite possibility). In that time, however long it may be, it's important to recognize and accept any mixed feelings you have about being single. Women who feel they are constantly on the defensive for taking dating slower sometimes try to make up for it by appearing extra confident. As one fortysomething woman told me, "I have to pretend I love being single and don't get lonely. Otherwise, it gets thrown in my face that it's my fault because I could be using dating services."

Being strong and resilient does not come from putting on a game face and tamping down your true feelings. It means knowing you can weather the emotional journey of feeling good one day about being single and lonely the next. You may not always like the journey, but you know that you'll be okay.

 ## Write it down: What's the hardest part of being single?

Make a list of all the downsides of being unmarried, being as thorough as possible. This is not the time to hold back, and no one is judging. Your list may include observations ("It's hard to walk down the sidewalk in the spring. It makes me sad seeing all the couples holding hands"); it may include anxieties ("I feel like a failure because I'm the only one of my friends who isn't married"). If you're having a hard time tuning in to them, think about events or experiences in the last few weeks that left you feeling upset. Did anyone call you recently and make you feel anxious about being single? Did you feel stuck in an uncomfortable situation?

Allow yourself to go deep, and release these feelings. You can handle it. When you're done, put your pen down and take a couple of deep breaths. What do you see?

Jean Marie, 30, told me: "It was being dragged by one of my 'baby' cousins to the dance floor for the bride's tossing of the bouquet at my other, younger cousin's wedding. It was like the parting of the seas—no women my age wanted to participate in the toss, even those who were unmarried! I'd like to think that they were all progressive and silently protesting the tradition, but it definitely felt more like no one my age wanted to be identified as 'single.' I ended up dodging the bouquet as it flew in my direction and let my cousin take it."

Lara, 38, told me that she woke up one day and realized she might not have a baby, and then she burst into tears. Rachel, 37, said her saddest moments are coming home and throwing frozen dinners in the microwave because it wasn't worth it to cook for only one. Samantha, 30, is sad that on top of having a rare eye illness, she doesn't know if she will meet a man who will be a good partner for her and can handle it. Vivienne, 40, is sad because her sexual peak is in full force and her "mojo" is being wasted.

The idea here is not to name your feelings so you can dwell in them and feel awful. Nor is it to get rid of them; they are not a bad case of acne. They are your feelings, and it's essential to give them room to breathe. They're not going to kill you. The only way they can do harm is if you deny their existence. Also, it's normal if this process seems strange and uncomfortable at first, especially if you're not used to feeling with intensity. But as you get better at recognizing and labeling your feelings, you will feel steadier on your feet. You will know who you are in a deeper way and understand your inner strength. That means that people can criticize your choices all they like; you are not going to get knocked down.

Tune in to your inner voice: How do I feel about my dating approach?

In order to remain strong—and not get undone by people telling you that your dating approach is all wrong—you will need to *keep* tuning in to your emotions and asking, "How do I feel about the steps I'm taking?" and "Am I being true to what works for me?" Then pay attention to what you hear back. This is not a one-time exercise, but rather something you can be doing once a week or so in order to continuously make sure you are making the best decisions for yourself.

Or, another signal that it's time to check in with your inner voice is if you notice any physical body aches or pain telling you that you're stressed. Rather than ignoring the fact that your jaw feels tight, for example, stop and ask your inner voice what's going on: "Oh, I think I'm clenching my teeth, which means I'm anxious. Let me take a sec and figure out what I am anxious about. Ah, it's that my baby sister is getting married and everyone is going to ask me how I feel about it. Then they're going to ask me about my dating life and what I'm doing to meet guys." There, it's out on the table. Take a deep breath and determine if you'd like to do something about the problem (such as find more opportunities ASAP to meet single men) or accept the feeling as human and go on with your day. Whatever you choose, paying attention to your feelings is a far better option than spending the day clueless with an aching, clenched jaw.

Write it down: What have you always wanted to try?

Write in your journal everything you've wanted to try but haven't had the opportunity to do yet. When you're done, circle the items in your list that you could make happen if you wanted to with the resources you have right now. Now, place a star by the ones you want to try first.

There are times when you'll likely be frustrated that no intriguing guy is calling to take you to dinner, and you're feeling itchy for male companionship. It's easy to get stuck in a doubt loop of "I'm never going to find someone" or "Something must be wrong with me." You're tired of going to the same restaurants or clubs with the same friends, and you're just waiting for something new and exciting to kick into gear. You've been patient. Now where the heck is it?

It ain't coming, sister, unless you make it happen. This is the time to try something from the list you just made, something you've always wanted to do but haven't had the money or courage or energy. We're talking about more than a night on the town; it's time to commit to something bold and ongoing. I'm not saying that learning how to rappel off a cliff or swing from a trapeze is going to make you forget about wanting a man, but it's going to knock you out of your rut and remind you of how much more there is to life than finding a guy. One of the best parts of being single is focusing on what *you* want to do rather than having to negotiate all the time with a boyfriend ("Okay, fine, this week we'll stay home and watch old *Star Trek* episodes again").

Grace, 26, took up contra dancing after she broke up with her last boyfriend. It's something she never thought she would do in a million years but as she put it, "I needed to do something that had nothing to do with my ex, made me feel good, and opened my eyes to possibilities." Jenna, 34, took herself on an international trip and loved the bold adventure of it. Snowboarding, art classes, pickup basketball, bonsai tree gardening . . . it's not about putting a Band-Aid on the situation ("maybe if I take up karate I'll forget to be lonely"), it's a decision to veer away from the blues and move toward joy.

Give yourself permission to change your mind.

You've already established you don't want to meet your future partner in a way that feels forced. The idea of telling your future child that you met your husband at a Lock & Key event makes you want to weep. But, as mentioned above, on the occasion that you get curious about what it might be like to try a new way to meet a man (who knows, maybe your horoscope advised you to take a love risk on the eve of the full moon), grant yourself permission. You don't have to tell anyone; or you can keep it on the down low. What's important is that you don't become so fixated on your all-natural approach that you won't try something new just to make a point. As I've heard Dr. Phil say over and over, "Do you want to be right or do you want to be happy?" Sometimes being happy is recognizing that you need to try things in your life you hadn't intended.

Lisa,* 42, for example, swore she would never do a speed-dating event because she found it "gross." I think her exact words were, "I would rather die alone in a house full of cats than set foot in one of those arenas of desperation!" But then something happened. A friend of hers announced she was going to try it, and without a hint of embarrassment or nervousness. According to Lisa, "My friend just took the whole thing so lightly, like, 'It'd be cool if I met a guy, but at the very least it'll be something wacky I tried.' I saw for the first time that maybe it wouldn't be so bad if you didn't judge the night based on landing a man, but rather just trying something new." So the next time her friend went, a few months later, Lisa tagged along. "I had sworn I'd never do this, but I told myself to get over it," she said. As it turned out, the men, said Lisa, were just as "nerdy and weird" as she predicted, but she had a great time. She connected with several of the women she was seated by, and even remained friends with a couple of them.

The point is not that you have to force yourself to do something you don't want to do. Rather, it's to stay open-minded and flexible. Make choices based on what feels right for you in the moment, not because you're committed to a theory.

Put away those flannels.

It's one thing to decide you aren't going out on the town with the explicit purpose of finding a guy. It's another thing to stay home every night, don your flannel pajamas, and watch repeats of *Lost* on TV while eating Chinese takeout. Janneane, 36, put it like this: "You just want to stay home because you're so frustrated with dating. When I was twenty, I didn't care that I was single. But I'm thirty-six now, and I'm tired of trying, and tired of being disappointed and trying to hold on to the hope that eventually the next one is going to be the one. It's easier to stay home."

Yes, it is easier to stay home every night where it's comfortable and safe. But that is not a way of letting things develop naturally;

it's not even *living*. It's pulling the blankets over your head and refusing to partake in the world. It's okay to go through bouts when you need to hole up and replenish. But this should be a short span of time and not a lifestyle choice. Dating expert David Wygant advises: "Life is in the field. Life is about enjoying the moment. Nothing happens for those who sit and wait. Challenge yourself to take action every day. You won't believe what is waiting out there for you!"

Sure, it may sound a little corny but, come on, the guy is right. Get out at least twice a week (yeah, I'm talking to you women who know every contestant's name on *Dancing with the Stars* from the last five seasons). That doesn't mean go out to find a guy; it just means leave your place with the intent of having fun. Check out event listings in your city or town and try something that strikes your fancy, something you never considered. Attend a lecture on Alfred Hitchcock, go midnight bowling with your girl-friends, sign up for a sushi-making class.

Or if you are hoping to meet a guy, you can certainly find off-the-cuff ways to do it. Try a pickup game of ultimate Frisbee at your recreation center, sign up for a midnight canoe ride at your local outdoor center, or sign up for a wine-tasting party. Your enjoyment won't ride on meeting Mr. Right, but at least meeting him is a possibility. If he is there, you know already you share something in common; if he's not, you're going to have a pleasant night regardless.

Pull that rabbit out of your drawer.

There is no reason to let your sexual desires fall by the wayside. Many single women over age twenty-five whom I interviewed have mixed feelings about how to meet their sexual needs. Many disliked the idea of hooking up with a man just to keep their sexual mojo going, because they hated the weird awkwardness afterward. "Hooking up at college used to be cool and I felt empowered by it," said one 45-year-old, "now it just feels like I'm disrespecting myself." Others agreed that they didn't want to have sex for the sake of sex anymore; they were craving real intimacy with a man.

That said, several women joked about being "born-again virgins" and "drying up" and "parts falling off." Denise, 39, told me that she'd been "celibate for a year—I'm not even kidding!" We are sexual creatures who crave physical intimacy and it shouldn't be denied. There's no point in waiting for the right man to unleash your wild side again, because you don't know when he's coming. Take a lesson from *Sex and the City*'s Samantha, who admitted readily to "polishing herself off once in a while," and figure out how to please yourself. It's good for you, it's good for your future man, and it's probably good for everyone who spends time with you.

You can skip ahead to the next section if you're a self-pleasing pro. If you're not, and your facing is burning red right now, keep reading. I highly recommend visiting a sex toy shop for women and checking out the selection of devices. You can do this online if you're feeling weird about others seeing you. But I will tell you this, I interviewed a manager of a Good Vibrations sex-toy boutique, a national chain, and the place was well lit, pleasant, and upbeat. Moreover, the female manager told me that all the staff is trained so they can help women understand what toys are best for what types of people. The whole experience is as easy as shopping for a cute purse.

If you're doubtful, consider this: It's downright bad for your health *not* to receive sexual excitement. Relationship expert Dr. Karen Gail Lewis agrees it's crucial that women take care of their sexual needs; otherwise, she said, she sees women end up engaging in overeating, too much drinking, too much smoking. She adds, "I think women have to be honest about the sexual feelings and say, 'I've got them. Now what am I going to do about them?'" So whether you start out with "a bubble bath and white wine" or just hop in bed and switch your toy to "On," indulge.

Keep your sensual mojo in place as well by celebrating your body. Sign up for salsa lessons, get a facial, read erotica, and maybe book monthly massages (every other month if your paycheck is slim). Don't think of these things as silly indulgences but rather as smart ways to keep you at your best. Hey, you always make sure your car is tuned up, your home appliances are up and running, and your job is on track. You need to make sure your sensuality is in good shape as well.

Allow friends to support you.

Many women told me the worst parts of being single are the moments of isolation and loneliness, and feeling like they have no one to lean on when they need it. What was interesting about this is that most of the women said they had at least one really supportive girlfriend in their life. But rather than call these girlfriends, they'd just bottle their feelings. The reason? Some didn't want to voice aloud their sadness because it would become more real; others worried their girlfriends would use this moment to push them into dating events instead of offering sympathy. Said one single woman: "I don't want to be told, 'Well, you wouldn't be alone if you'd put yourself out there more.' I just want emotional support."

You don't have to grin and bear it during these hard times. This is the exact time to call on a friend for company and possibly a gentle pep talk. Come on, wouldn't you happily be there for your friend if she were feeling down? Seek out extra hugs from pals, and let them know what you need, even if it's just time together without any talking, or the opportunity to express your thoughts without being given advice. Give them a chance.

In the meantime, continue to write in your journal and treat it like a confidante. So many women keep a diary through their preteen years and that's the last time they ever record their feelings. One of my friends always scoffs when I recommend journaling: "I don't have time to do that every day!" You don't have to; it's not meant to be another task in your life. Think of it as a trusted friend who is always there for you and will never say the wrong thing. Use as needed.

Realize the outside commentary is just noise.

Here you are sorting through your feelings and staying in tune with the ups and downs of what you need on different days. You're staying as flexible as you can with your attitude, and taking risks while trying to meet many of your own needs. You're working to feel centered and strong. The *last* thing you need is people telling you you'd be so much happier if you would do *x*, *y*, and *z* to find a man ("You must join Chemistry.com" or "Go with a professional matchmaking service" or "Call my cousin, what do you have to lose?!").

When you politely say no thank-you, they look at you like you have offended *them* in some way. "Well," they might say, "fine, but you're not going to meet anyone at home!" (which is when you have to stifle yourself from asking, "Oh, really? I was hoping a parade of eligible men would march through my living room"). You'd really like to respond: "Why is this so important to you?" and "How about you concentrate on your own life?"

Here are other comments single women say they are sick to death of hearing:

- "You need to get out there and should lower your standards!"
- "It's high time you were married."
- "What's wrong with you?"
- "You are not getting any younger, you know."
- "Well, you've got to kiss a lot of frogs!"
- And the most popular: "If you weren't so picky, you'd be with someone."

Lauren, 28, confessed she's absolutely sick of people saying, "You are just 'too picky.' Telling that to a woman who is searching for a true life partner is like telling an ambitious and competent graduate that their career goals or dreams are 'too high.' Society would never say that about the latter. Such a thing would be taboo."

Janneke, 33, said she was flabbergasted when she was told, "You need to lower your standards," by a married guy. "I was so offended at the time that I didn't have the quickness to tell him what I should've said . . . 'Oh, is that what your wife did when she met you?'"

First of all, understand that people who are confident and happy in their lives don't need to accuse or attack you for your personal choices. They can let you make your own decisions, as they would, and wish you well. People who go on the attack are like schoolyard bullies, who typically try to bring you down to make themselves feel better. Or there is something about the choices you are making that may be making them feel defensive or threatened about their own relationships.

Said one interviewee, "My friends who date online complain about it all the time, but then they tell me that I'm making a huge mistake by not doing it too. When I say, 'But you hate it,' they tell me that at least they are out there trying. It's weird logic to me. It's like saying, 'I'm trying this system that doesn't work and makes me feel bad; you should do it too so we can be in it together.' Here's another idea: How about neither of us do it?"

If you can remember, in the heat of the moment, that they are acting from their own insecurities and motives—and not from a place of really understanding you—the comments won't do any emotional damage. They may continue to be annoying but they won't get under your skin so much.

Tell the peanut gallery to pipe down.

If it's your close friend making offensive comments, know that she probably is genuinely concerned about your well-being and not just being a judgmental jerk. To this friend, it's best to say calmly, "You're a good friend and I appreciate your concern, but what I really need from you is your support and friendship—not tips on how to meet a man." If she comes back with, "I'm only trying to help," tell her that you really understand that but what would help is a listening ear or just having fun together and taking a break from talking about men. Assure your friend you adore her and want the friendship to stay strong, and that's why you're telling her the truth.

If we're talking about an officemate, third cousin, or not-so-close friend who keeps e-mailing you clippings about where to meet men, try saying, "Thanks, I get enough suggestions from my mom," or "Thanks for thinking of me, but I'm all set on the dating front." If they keep sending you stuff, tell them that you'd appreciate them knocking it off, and where appropriate, deleting all of their contact info (see you later, Facebook friend!). Enough is enough, and when you tell someone their behavior makes you feel bad, the expectation is that they need to stop immediately. If they can't, they don't get the pleasure of spending time with you.

No matter who the buttinsky is you're dealing with, remind yourself that their words have nothing to do with how you're really doing. Their problem with your dating style should remain *their* problem, not yours. Who knows why they are so desperate to couple you off? Maybe it's to validate their own relationship decision, or maybe they're just bored and need a project. Well, they can find a different project. You've got a life to live.

Schedule the Mom talk: Ask her to stop handing out your contact info to single men.

You have the mom who just can't help herself (apparently) from striking up a conversation with any non-ring-wearing man she meets out in public. She'll cozy up to him, ask him a few questions, and slip in the fact that she has a single daughter who's gorgeous. Maybe your mom even, sweet horror, takes out a photo of you and shows it to him, and even slips him your digits.

For those (all three of you) who appreciate your mom's pimp-like efforts, good for you. But for those who would like to strangle your mom, it's time to talk. First, understand that your mother is not actually trying to torment you or sell you like a piece of meat. In her eyes she is taking active steps to make you happier. That doesn't mean her actions are appropriate, but they are well intentioned. Let's put an end to those good intentions.

"Mom," you say calmly, "I understand that you'd like me to find a guy to fall in love with. I would like the same thing. But I need you to stop giving my phone number to men without asking me if it's okay." If she asks you what's wrong about it, go ahead and let her know it makes you feel like a product sold on the market and you'd like it to stop.

Then set the boundaries. Maybe it's okay for her to give your number to men who fit certain criteria (like guys under the age of sixty, say). Maybe it's all right with you only for her to give you the name and phone number of single men so you can do a little Google research on your own. Maybe you'd prefer she butt out of your love life altogether and never give your number out. That's fine too. But she can't guess the rules, so it's up to you to explain them and let her know if the rules change.

 ## In case of emergency:
Say no to home for the holidays.

Whether or not you're able to straighten things out with your mom, you've still got the rest of the family to contend with. This is most prevalent during the holidays—like those special moments when family gets together and makes you feel like a complete loser for not being married. Don't make the mistake of thinking you're stuck with this dreary situation until you find a partner to bring home with you. You are a grown woman with a say in how you're treated. Tell family members who grill you about your dating status that you're doing fine without a boyfriend, thank you. If they keep meddling—and it's starting to feel like a group sport—say good night to everyone and leave. You are under no obligation to stick it out, and there are no medals of honor for making it through the whole evening. Next year, consider passing on the get-together and creating a new ritual with people who lift your spirits. Invite a few like-minded single women over for a potluck dinner. Or attend a holiday gathering with a friend's (less judgmental) family. Plan a solo trip somewhere exotic, or volunteer somewhere where you'll be truly appreciated. Celebrate the fact that you can no longer be forced by your folks into situations that leave you feeling terrible. You call the shots now.

 KEEP YOUR NEST EGG SAFE

The good news is you're probably saving a good sum of cash by not investing in pricey matchmakers and dating services. That said, it's essential to keep your financial life stable, and being financially independent takes pressure off of *needing* to find Mr. Right. Here's a tip that comes from money editor Martin Brown

(continued)

at Single Minded Women: Divide whatever you have as your savings nest egg—$3,000 or $300,000—into three approximately even portions. Martin suggests placing one-third in municipal bonds, one-third in money markets or treasury notes, and one-third into a more aggressive investment such as a stock growth fund. In this last third, adjust the investment to match your tolerance for risk, he suggests.

 ## 5 MORE REASONS TO AVOID INTERNET DATING

1. No more men who claim in their profile they are just shy of six feet when in actuality they'd need a step stool to kiss you good night.

2. It's obnoxious receiving a "wink" from someone online; can you really not spare the two minutes to craft an actual e-mail?

3. It's impossible to tell if the baseball hat he's wearing in his pic proves he's super laid-back or super bald.

4. No more contending with guys who check off "complicated" to define their relationship status. You're in one or you're not.

5. Seems suspicious when you see he's cropped out someone from his profile pic—an ex? Current wife?

REMINDER CHECKLIST

1. Know if you're self-aware—or scared. It's important to know that you're making decisions with intention.

2. Write it down: What's the hardest part of being single?

3. Tune in to your inner voice: How do I feel about my dating behavior?

4. Write it down: What have you always wanted to try?

5. Open your mind to changing your mind. Remember that you are allowed to try a dating event whenever you feel like it.

6. Put away those flannels, honey. It's one thing to avoid singles events and another to hibernate at home; make plans to get out of the house.

7. Pull that rabbit out of your drawer. Make sure you aren't denying yourself sexual pleasure while you're single.

8. Allow friends to support you. Call your close friends when you're feeling down and let them know what you need.

9. Realize the outside commentary is just noise. Remind yourself that only you know what works best for you.

10. Tell the peanut gallery to pipe down. If you're getting a lot of lip from others about your love life, ask them politely and firmly to stop.

11. Schedule the Mom talk. Tell your mother to stop giving out your name and phone number to every single man she meets.

12. In case of emergency: Say no to home for the holidays.

PART TWO

Experiencing Conflicting Feelings About Being Single

💜

Mix. Put in blender. Shake. Pour. Repeat.

Or: Help! I'm mixed-up about how

I feel about being single.

4

The Princess in Waiting

Definition: You are still waiting to be rescued by a prince who sure is taking his royal time.

Pop Quiz

When your niece puts *Cinderella* on the DVD player, you automatically:

- **A** Grab a bucket of popcorn and join her; you love this story!
- **B** Flee the room before she can yell, "Watch this part!"
- **C** Lecture her about the trappings of the "rescue fantasy."

If you answered A, this chapter is for you.

JENNA'S STORY

"I always thought Mr. Right would sweep into my life and everything would pull together," says Jenna,* 29. "All of the annoyances in my life—paying off law school loans and fighting with my mother and dealing with my weight issues—would somehow re-solve themselves."

When Jenna first started dating Aaron, it was just like her fantasy. "I was giddy at the idea of seeing him and my heart would race when we got together." But since the endorphins have calmed down, Jenna isn't sure if Aaron is right for her. "It's become kind of humdrum," she said. "He goes to work, I go to work. We have dinner and talk about what happened in the day. I love him, but there is no pizzazz anymore." It doesn't help that she's still dealing with law school loans, lost a chunk of her 401(k) when the economy tanked, and is still trying to keep her weight under control. For Jenna, who's been living with Aaron for a few months now, it's just not what she expected. "He's really good to me. But, I don't know, I wonder if this is really my Prince Charming."

Stage of Singlehood

You were the girl among your friends who would have been voted "most likely to wear a poofy, white wedding gown." You memorized all your favorite lines from fairy tales and romantic movie classics, and have dreamt a thousand times about a hand-some prince popping into your life and carrying you off into the sunset. *Sigh*. You know these stories aren't real (you are not clini-cally insane), but you have been carrying them around in your head for so long that it's hard to feel all that thrilled by new dating prospects or your current boyfriend. Yes, he's attractive and a good person, but where's the magic and mystery? You are simply not living the fairy-tale life you envisioned. Aren't you supposed to at least light up when the right guy walks into the room?

The Great News

You may be feeling kind of shafted that your latest date or serious boyfriend is not the romantic lead you spent your childhood dreaming about (there's no swashbuckling, no sweeping you off your feet), but life is about to get sweeter. Here's why: You are suffering from holding on to sky-high expectations of what a man can bring to your life. This means you're disappointed on a regular basis, and always questioning whether the men in your life are good enough. No one can match the glamour and sex appeal of your fantasy man. But if you are open to revising your criteria, you will experience deeper, more meaningful relationships with men— instead of feeling constantly gypped.

This is also an excellent opportunity to learn how to rescue yourself so you're not so fixated with the idea of a guy doing it for you. On the surface, saving yourself might not seem as tantalizing as having Mr. Tall, Dark, and Handsome do the job. But it is time for you to know, and to trust, that you can take care of yourself. Yes, you'll need people to help along the way, but the *most* reliable person to bail you out of a sticky situation is you. How lucky that you are not a fairy-tale princess (without resources, stuck in a dire home situation, living at a time where women *needed* a prince to yank them out of a bad scenario). You can get your own life on track—and continue making necessary adjustments when it's veering off track. By following the steps in this chapter you'll feel emboldened to take on the role and, hopefully, be excited by the possibilities that open as a result.

ACTION ITEMS

See the princess dream for what it is.

The hardest part of your journey may be acknowledging that happily ever after, the way so many girls dreamt about it, is not real. Who could blame you if you've been secretly holding on to the idea in your heart? With the pretty gowns, royal weddings, white horses, and friendly chattering animals, who wouldn't be swept away? But here's the thing: The stories never moved past the part where the princess kisses her man at the wedding. End of story.

We never witness the next day when the princess wanted to punch her handsome prince in the throat because he snored like a jackhammer; when the newlyweds had to figure out who was going to pay the plumber and whether they'd have a joint checking account. We never heard about the fact that the princess's mother-in-law called constantly to find out when her daughter-in-law was planning to get pregnant, leaving the princess in tears of infuriation.

The huge disservice of these fairy tales was that they created a relationship model about as substantial as fluff. As Anthony Vitale, the owner of a Boston hair salon put it, "I don't know who wrote those stories, but I know it wasn't guys. Men don't think like that." He has a point. It's hard to shed expectations for the perfect prince, even though we know *logically* he doesn't exist. Some women still crave it in an "if only" way. Anthony, who has listened to hundreds of women in his salon chair over the years complaining about men, went on to say, "I think a lot of women want that fairy-tale thing and get stuck on that, and it just kills them that they don't get to have it. Girls are brought up like princesses. But unfortunately boys aren't brought up to be princes. We're brought up to be kings. And that's just the thing. Kings and princesses don't really mix." In other words, healthy, well-adjusted men do not want to spend their lives fixing your life.

So if part of you has been clinging to the fantasy, consciously or not, it's time to ask yourself if you want to stay attached to something you can never have. Is a lifetime of longing really enough for you? Or do you want to figure out how to let go of the old fantasy once and for all and find a new obtainable goal? If the latter appeals to you—or at least peaks your curiosity—read on.

 ## Write it down: Why are you attached to the Cinderella fantasy?

Spend ten to fifteen minutes writing in your journal about your desire for the fairy-tale ending and why it's so important to you. You can write a list of reasons if there is more than one; or write in depth if there is one main reason. Then read over your answer and see what you can glean from it.

It may be that you are craving an endorphin rush because life is a little flat right now. Maybe you have been living on autopilot: wake up, get dressed, have breakfast, go to work, come home, make dinner, eat, check e-mail, call friends, watch TV, off to bed. The next day, you wake up and do it all over again in an endless loop. If you don't have a boyfriend, maybe you feel like you keep seeing the same guys over and over on online dating sites. If you are with a guy, you feel like you're having the same talks and bickering about the same issues. *Is this all there is?* Getting stuck in a rut happens to just about everyone at some point. Or maybe you're tied to the fairy tale because it represents something deeper—the opportunity to escape from a relationship or situation that is trapping you. What you really seek is freedom.

Many of the women I interviewed confessed to holding on to a princess fantasy:

April,* 44, admitted, "For a long time I thought the answer to my prayers would be for an amazing man to sweep me off my feet. I have a boyfriend, but I assumed there was something wrong with him because I was feeling depressed, and assumed he had something to do with it. But what I needed was a change in my life. I was working from home for years and feeling isolated and bored. I would fantasize about a perfect man knocking on my door and introducing himself; then we'd fall in love and I'd break up with my boyfriend. But time passed and that didn't happen, and I realized I was going to have to try something new. I ended up taking a job at an office with a bunch of creative people and my life changed. I feel so much happier now. And not surprising, things have picked up with my boyfriend. My happiness put back the spark in the relationship for both of us."

As 27-year-old Naz put it, "I think the reason that fairy tales are so successful is because girls are looking for an out. Take Ariel from *The Little Mermaid*. She is a struggling with her dad and the feeling of being closed up and wanting bigger, more open, wider spaces, to steal from the Dixie Chicks. But the truth is that a lot of girls—and a lot of women—want to break out of this life. The problem is, the way you are supposed to do this is to find a guy to rescue you. There are surely other ways to break free!"

"The reason the fairy tale was appealing for me as a kid was because I needed someone to save me," says Keisha,* 43. "My father was kind of a tyrant, and my mother didn't do much to stand up to him on behalf of my sisters or me. I wasn't in any position to tell him to back off, and I felt powerless. So after school, while my mom was at work, I would watch *Cinderella* over and over, with her mean stepmother and stepsisters, and I'd wait for the part when the prince came to take Cinderella away and marry her. I convinced myself that if I was pretty enough and kind enough, a prince would come and take me away too. That is what I prayed for."

What is it for you? Do you connect with wanting a knight in shining armor to fill the void in your life? Was there something about your own upbringing that left you longing to be saved? Are you wanting to shake things up in your life but don't know how to start?

 ## Tune in to your inner voice: Do these stories resonate personally?

Find a quiet spot, close your eyes, and ask whether you relate to the desire for freedom, excitement, or escape. See what surfaces, you may be surprised. If you sense there is something deep but just can't access it, don't beat up on yourself. Tune in to your inner voice for a few weeks to see if something shifts. If not, that's okay; consider seeking out a trusted therapist who can guide you through old issues so they stop getting in your way. You deserve to put this to rest so you can find true (obtainable) happiness.

Determine whether you're simply pining for help.

There's so much women are in charge of these days: our finances, career, investments, education, social calendars, office politics, and so on. We know that we are lucky to have all of these choices at our disposal (thanks to the women who fought for us to have choices) and control so many elements of our lives. But let's face it, it's tiring. Perhaps the real reason we want a prince is that we just need a break.

Hey, there's a reason that fairy tales and romantic film classics remain immensely popular. It's hard not to love the notion of a prince—or anyone—saving us from drudgery. Sure, the look of drudgery has changed over the years. Cinderella was sweeping cinders from around the fireplace while her stepmother barked orders. Today, it's working long hours at our demanding jobs while our bosses bark orders; trying to keep up with school or business loans; worrying about our shrinking 401(k) plans; dealing with computer meltdowns and attempts at data recovery; and refinancing our mortgages. *Modern-day drudgery*. In an e-zine article called "Stress Management for Women," L. John Mason, Ph.D., author of *Guide to Stress Reduction*, points out, "I believe that everyone is experiencing higher levels of stress in the Information Age. The pace of change has accelerated to the point where we are forced to confront more changes and faster-paced changes in this day and age than at any time in the past." All of us are essentially rushing to keep up.

For many women, the idea of a prince sweeping into their lives and taking charge is bliss. In the fantasy, your dream guy might say, "You rest, I will fill out our taxes this year," or "You work so hard, let me treat you to a fabulous night out," or "Don't worry about finding someone to fix the leaky roof; I'll do it." Where *is* that guy? If you're in dating mode, it's not like you're going to ask a guy you don't know well to help you get your life on track. Nor does a steady boyfriend mean you're going to get all of your obligations met. That leaves you to take care of it.

Karen, 33, wants a man to paint her walls. Vivienne, 40, sometimes yearns for a macho man, "not a guy who is violent or abusive, but the kind of guy who will say, 'Here's what we're doing tonight.'" Mae, 27, wants a guy to fix her leaking faucet because "it's so friggin' expensive having someone come in to do it; plus I don't want some strange man I don't even know coming up to my place!" Max, 44, wants a guy to carry packages for her from the lobby of her apartment building up the four flights to her walkup. "It's not that I can't do it," she adds. "It would just be nice if someone could help me once in a while."

 ## Write it down: What obligation(s) would you most like to trash?

Spend fifteen to twenty minutes writing in your journal what you would do if a prince swept in today and said he would rescue you. What would you request (or what would you delete from your Outlook express calendar)? Moving heavy furniture? Helping with housework? Taking part in planning major life events? Shoveling the driveway? Fixing your computer? Let go and let your mind wander about what your fantasy looks like. How would it feel to get this obligation off your back once and for all? In truth, once you start to lessen your stress load, you may find that the fantasy of a prince showing up is really beside the point.

Be a queen, and delegate.

First question: What can you do to eliminate the tasks on your list? If you're thinking "nothing," think again. Today there are advisers and experts on just about everything you could ever ask for. Is there some amount of money you could allot to taking care of the problem? I was raised by a pragmatic mom who sees all problems as "those you can throw money at and those you can't." She's not a notably wealthy woman, but she does know that for a couple hundred bucks, a lot of hassles can be fixed quickly. It's really about women believing they deserve to spend money on their own behalf. So rather than dreaming of your royal highness to help, see if you can delegate the responsibility to a pro. Who is to say Prince Charming would even have a clue as to what you should do in terms of your Roth IRA or how to fix the broken microwave?

If you are dealing with a limited budget, that just means you are going to have to be resourceful. Start with Craigslist (www.craigslist.org), the megapopular website where people list goods and services typically for discounted prices. If you find an appealing deal on a service that you need, ask the provider for a few references to check so you don't get scammed. I have found on Craigslist amazing handymen, plumbers, and electricians who I have used for years. Another approach is to barter, by which you swap services with someone. This could be as simple as your doing your friend's taxes in exchange for her helping you paint your kitchen. Or maybe your friend brings over a homemade dinner a couple of times a week and you teach her how to use Photoshop. Let your friends, family, and colleagues know what services you're seeking and what you could offer in exchange. The goal is to use your skills and abilities to get rid of items on your calendar that you dread.

By the way, the original fairy tales (pre-Disney) were actually about the main character figuring out how to save his- or herself. Says Maria Tatar, professor of folklore and mythology at Harvard University, "I think one thing that Disney has done is to capitalize on the marriage theme in fairy tales. In the earlier tales often it was about getting through and surviving. There were stories about romantic matches, but what was really important was getting through the day, turning the tables on oppressors, and that kind of thing. Disney very early on discovered that they could tap into what I think is now called the princess syndrome." If you want to envision yourself as a princess, imagine being a *pre-Disney* princess—a woman who can get herself out of harsh situations. Sure, there's romance in her life, but it's not because she can't hack it in the world.

Look for real men, not cartoon princes.

Now that you are standing on your own two feet, it's time to change your approach to dating. Most likely in the past you've gone out with perfectly good guys and dismissed them after one or two dates because they didn't live up to your fantasy. Maybe you didn't like their job or the type of dog they owned or their penchant for wearing sandals. So they got the ax. These were not men you could *swoon* over. On the other hand, you might have tossed a really great guy back into the sea because he didn't live up to your vision of perfection. And it's likely that some smart woman has paired off with him by now who didn't care what kind of dog he owned, while gently persuading him to lose the sandals.

Point being: If you really want to find intimacy with a man, you're going to have to reevaluate and adjust your criteria (see "Readjust your 'wanted' list" in chapter 1 for guidance on this).

Ellen,* 34, is someone who eventually tossed aside her prince dream when she saw it was not getting her anywhere. She admits, "I was looking for a guy for years who would dazzle me with jewelry and sing me love songs and treat me like a queen. Oh, and he had to be good-looking. But at some point, actually when I turned 33, I realized that I was going to end up alone because this guy I was seeking did not exist. It was only when I let go of the fantasy and started dating different types of guys and giving them a real chance that I found my current boyfriend. He does not look like a prince on the outside but he does treat me like a queen, and what's more, I find myself wanting to put him on a pedestal because he's so decent. I wasted so much time looking for perfection."

Add your own bits of glamour.

If it's not just the abundance of tasks but a general malaise you're feeling, you can fix that right now. If you're bored out of your gourd at work, find out if there are new challenges or opportunities you can take on. Will your employer pay for you to take some kind of educational training? If it's simply the wrong job, start perusing for a new one. For a quick fix, sign up for a class in something you always wanted to learn about. Volunteer. Join a running club, take a class in bartending, comb the beach and start a collection of exotic seashells. Waiting for a man to undo your boredom is not a practical or sustaining solution, and you could be waiting for a long time.

If romance and passion are what you seek (you can't stand one more night of takeout and TV repeats with your boyfriend), make it happen. Invite your man over for a candlelit dinner. Surprise him with a picnic in the park. Send him a love note sprayed with perfume. Tell him it's "massage night," and he gets to go first. Lip-lock him in the kitchen when he's not expecting it. No, you aren't responsible for creating all of the romance in your relationship, but you are responsible for initiating *some*, and you might as well get the ball rolling. Hopefully, he'll enjoy it so much that he'll take your lead. If not, you may have to tell him that it's important to you and give him specific ideas while he finds his romantic way. Thank him when he does and encourage him to do more by telling him how great it felt. If he still won't take it up a notch in the romance department—even though you have talked to him about how important it is to the relationship—this may not be your guy.

See the fantasy in hindsight.

It may help to recall that even in fairy tales, the princes we grew up fantasizing over were devoid of personality. Think about it. What made Prince Eric different than Prince Charming? Can you even name the prince in *Beauty and the Beast*? (It's Adam. I had to look it up.) As fairy-tale expert Maria Tatar, mentioned previously, put it, "Disney gives us this cardboard prince, a sort of Ken-like figure with no personality whatsoever." Maybe the princes were like Barbie's Ken doll companion, there to decorate Barbie's home and allow us to project whatever personality we wanted on him; he was a blank slate for our fantasies.

For several of the women I interviewed, their fantasy man was less Disney and more Hollywood. Their princes were strong leading men who desired their women and stopped at nothing to win them over:

Robin, 33, claimed, "Oh, yeah, there's that line, 'You don't want to be in love, you want to be in love in the movies.' I think that in the old movies, they had such good scripts. I really like wit in a man, and it's not very present now. But I love a guy who can deliver a comeback like Spencer Tracy, and I want that in my boyfriend."

Shoshanna,* 41, said, "My boyfriend is a really nice guy and he's cute, but he has some habits that are intolerable. He refuses to pick up his clothes off our floor; he talks so loud when he's on the phone that I can't hear the TV, and he will stand there and fart while I'm in the room and think it's funny. It's not, it's gross. God, why can't he be debonair like men in the movies?"

Yes, in the movies and in books, leading men know just what to say and how to say it. They look you square in the eye and announce, "I was born when you kissed me. I died when you left me. I lived a few weeks while you loved me" (thanks, Humphrey Bogart, in *In a Lonely Place*), and "It seems right now that all I've ever done in my life is making my way here to you" (Clint Eastwood, in *The Bridges of Madison County*). *Ahhh.*

Of course, these men had scriptwriters crafting every word. Do you know a guy who says witty sweet nothings like this out of the blue? I don't. Do you know men who leap off tall buildings in a single bound and sweep you up in their arms? Yeah, me neither. I love being in the company of men. In general, I think they're funny, they bring new ideas and attitudes to light and they challenge us to new ways of thinking. They're interesting to talk to and can help us better figure out our own perspectives. They're also great for flirting, sexual acts, and cuddling. But they're not perfect (much like ourselves).

Stop comparing your guy to a blank slate you can project your fantasies onto. Far better than blank slates are real men who support us through the ups and downs of life. Sure, there's something hot about the idea of a prince fighting off dragons and refilling our wine goblets at the royal ball. But dragons and goblets aren't exactly a part of our modern daily lives. What is *relevant* today is a good man who takes care of the dinner plans after a long day, knows how to make you laugh, and is prepared to do the work that goes into creating a healthy relationship. Maybe they don't bring the most eloquent and witty lines, but they care for you and allow you to care for them.

Go in search of new models.

One way to begin adjusting your expectations is to seek out the female relatives and friends who you consider to be in strong, healthy relationships. Ask them about the ups/downs of their husband, and what compromises they may have had to make over the years. What did they love about their man? What drives them crazy about him? What were some of the adjustments that they had to make in the name of their relationship? Let them know you're reassessing your own expectation levels. This is not to say that you're going to have the exact same criteria that these women have, but it's a good way to start seeing that solid relationships don't hinge on a perfect man and they can't be the solution to your problems.

"I told my friend that my relationship was nothing like the way I pictured it," said Stacy,* 38. "And she said, 'Yeah, none of us picture working on our relationships when we're kids. We just think relationships work out magically. But then you see that in any good relationship, you both work on it to keep it moving forward.' She wasn't judgmental and didn't tell me to grow up. She just said those wise words, and I realized that I hadn't done the work. When things started getting routine with my boyfriend, I blamed him. I didn't see that I could have worked too to bring in the romance."

Cindy, 45, learned from her friends that "women have gotten kind of crazy with what we expect from relationships. We want our partner to be our *everything*. And that's just impossible. Nobody can be everything!"

Vivienne, 39, says she has learned from other women friends that meeting someone else can't alter everything you are (your history, your personal experiences). It's not like you suddenly become this entirely different person because you're in love. She said, "If anything, love complicates things; it makes you question everything you are and everything you do. Love can be hard and even painful, so this whole 'I meet someone and I get married, everything's going to be perfect' is such a scam."

Read well-reviewed self-help books on creating healthy relationships, such as *How to Improve Your Marriage Without Talking About It* by Patricia Love and *The Seven Principles for Making Marriage Work* by John Gottman and Nan Silver. You don't have to be married to benefit from the advice and ideas in these books. Highlight sentences that call out to you and offer new insights about realistic expectations. Take notes on meaningful thoughts or perspectives you want to remember. Put effort into this because it is truly some of the most important research you'll ever do.

Think of it as a way to sample different relationship styles and see which ones resonate for you. How will you know? When you hear about marital styles that make your mind say yes, listen to that voice. Use those strategies and start crafting a vision of your own healthy relationship. Know that your criteria may change as you try it out, and that's okay, it should. Creating a strong, thriving relationship is a work in progress between both partners.

Schedule the Mom talk: Learn more about her own relationship expectations.

Given how much relationship info we tend to take in from our own mothers, it's worth exploring what messages your mom may have taught you about Mr. Right and being rescued. Was she someone who you saw as needing rescue when you were a child? If so, why? What about now? What would your mother have to say about her relationship dreams and whether they have been met?

Tell her you've been thinking about your relationship patterns and what you expect from men. Ask her what she saw when she met your dad and what she sees in him now. If they are still together, ask her what has held them together all these years and what sacrifices she has made. If your parents are divorced, ask what went wrong with the marriage. You may have talked about this in the past, but it will likely be a different conversation now.

Hopefully, she'll open up to you and you'll realize whether

you've been influenced by your mother's relationship(s) with men. Don't blame her or criticize her for the choices that she made. Instead, see if you can empathize with her and figure out what you would like to do similarly to her and what you will do differently. Remember, you have the choice to do things differently— although it's not always easy.

Helene Rothschild, counselor and founder of the nonprofit educational program Joyful Living, says, "Are we doomed to repeat our parents' dysfunctional patterns? We probably are, unless we raise our self-esteem and become conscious of how we are choosing our loved ones." She suggests that you "notice the similarities between the patterns of your relationships and that of your parents. Then, have the courage to do what you need to, in order to heal dysfunctional patterns, so that you can enjoy healthy relationships."

Decide whether your current guy is a good fit.

If you have spent years with impossibly high expectations for boyfriends, it may feel strange looking at him with fresh eyes. You are now comparing him to a real person and not Prince Charming. Does your guy seem like a worthwhile partner, warts and all? I like this statement I found in an article called "Are Your Expectations Too High or Too Low?" on eHarmony's website: "We all have certain flaws, and creating a healthy and fulfilling relationship is about finding a like-minded person who offers much of what we're looking for in a partner, and then compromising and negotiating on the issues where differences occur. So stop looking for the ideal mate, and begin searching for someone you can see yourself creating a strong and long-lasting relationship with."

Tune in to your inner voice: Should you turn a new page or end the story?

Find a quiet location, close your eyes, and ask yourself whether your boyfriend is the right person for you now that you've shifted your attitude. Are you excited to test-drive some of your new insights with your guy or turned off by the idea? Can you trust him? Do you love him as the man he is right now?

If you feel that your imperfect man is someone you want to create a long-lasting relationship with, talk to him about the changes you want to make. Take accountability for expecting too much from him, and let him know that you intend to search for ways to make your own life better rather than always relying on him to do it. He will be thrilled. In an article called "Men Sick of Women's Fairy-tale Fantasies," an anonymous male writer for Your Tango (yourtango.com) claims, "Men do not want to be princes. Princes are born into success, men make their own. We want women who share that same ethic, however it is success is defined. It's just not sexy to date a helpless princess." This is also a good time to tell him that you'd like both of you to work on restoring the razzle-dazzle in your romance and breaking out of the rut. Give him a suggestion for the first outing and commit to a date on the calendar.

If after much deliberation you realize that while you do need to change your expectations, your boyfriend is not the right man for you, then you should probably end things sooner rather than later. Hopefully, if there is sadness in the idea of a breakup, there is also hope in finding a more rewarding relationship down the road with the right person and for the right reasons. During your breakup period, you will have the opportunity to do more soul-searching, look at why you chose your boyfriend, what you were hoping he would bring to your life, why it didn't work out, and what you want from the next man. (For help with this, read the section "Readjust your 'wanted' list" in chapter 1.) In any case, enjoy this new time of delegating drudgery where possible and finding new ways to bring change to your life. Carry your own internal shield and sword, feel the strength of your new resolution, and celebrate every time you find a way to take care of something instead of depending on a man to do it. Add bits of glamour to your life when it's lacking (whether it's taking yourself to the opera or enjoying a night on the town with friends or booking a trip to Venice or walking through a local art museum). Forget the white horse; grab your purse, spray yourself with a hit of perfume, don a funky outfit, and see where the day takes you. The princesses in fairy tales didn't have the means to do this without a prince; you do. So take advantage of how much the world opens when you take charge.

 ## In case of emergency: Set up a health team who can rescue you.

If part of the reason you've stayed with your current beau is that you worry about who will take care of you when you're sick or get old, there's another option. Create a backup health-support team. Chances are you have a best friend (or a few close friends) who would come to your rescue when needed—if not a sibling, a parent, cousin, or other family member. They may not lawfully have to agree to take care of you in sickness and in health, but I can't name one married friend who wouldn't figure out how to help a close single friend in dire need the second they hung up the phone. If you can't say that about at least one or two of your friends, it may be time to assess the people you're hanging out with (or what kind of friend you yourself have been).

Talk to your girlfriends, both single and married. Go out for coffee with them and tell them that you worry about the possibility of being sick, injured, and/or needing some other kind of medical help. Let them know that it would comfort you if you knew they could be part of a support team to help you in duress. Notice I didn't say they could be *the* person, but part of a small team. The reality is that it can be tough for a woman with kids to commit to being the solo person to help you (child in dire need comes before friend in need), but asking them to be part of a support group is reasonable; likely they will want you to do the same for them. After all, husbands aren't always around at the time of need either, right? Be specific about what you are asking from them, such as being your emergency contact, taking care of your pets if you are hospitalized, accompanying you to take notes during a medical consultation, bringing you to the ER if necessary. Again, you can divvy up these requests among a couple of friends. Knowing you have taken these precautions in advance will help remove the "what if" worries from your present.

$ PROTECT YOUR MOST PRECIOUS POSSESSION WITH INSURANCE

Another way to keep yourself from needing rescue is to take care of your health. If you're without insurance—and waiting to see how the health-care overhaul will shake out—pay for catastrophic health insurance at the very least. That way, you know you're not going to go bankrupt if, God forbid, you get seriously ill and face massive medical bills. The way this type of insurance works is that you pay a low premium each month and then a higher deductible, should something happen (but not so high that you get financially wiped out).

Women who saved themselves

If the idea of spending a lifetime fixing your own problems seems daunting, take inspiration from the three amazing women described below, whose lives were at stake.

In 2008, Allena Hansen, 57, was walking her dogs in Caliente, California, when a brown bear attacked her. In spite of severe lacerations, Allena somehow kept her cool, escaped from the bear (whom she called a "bully"), and drove herself to a nearby fire station. From there, she was airlifted to UCLA Medical Center, treated, and released. Many said it was a miracle that this hundred-pound petite woman was able to fight off a 150-pound bear!

In 2007, a 78-year-old retiree in Berlin saved herself and others from major injuries after her taxi driver suddenly died of a heart attack on Germany's autobahn highway. The woman, who was in the front passenger seat, reached across and yanked the car out of gear, then pulled the hand brake. The car veered to a stop three hundred yards further, and the woman got out of the cab, unharmed.

In 2009, Kortni Peek lost control of her car on an icy road in Indiana, with her two daughters, ages eight months and two, in the backseat. The car swerved off the road and into a pond, becoming almost completely submerged. Kortni managed to unstrap both girls from their seat belts, push them and then herself out the window, and then swim all three of them to safety.

 REMINDER CHECKLIST

1. See the princess dream for what it is. The first step to finding happiness is acknowledging that the fairy tale isn't real.

2. Write it down: Why are you attached to the Cinderella fantasy?

3. Determine whether you're simply pining for help. Realize that it may be a relief from stress you're seeking more than a fairy-tale prince.

4. Write it down: What obligation(s) would you most like to trash?

5. Be a queen, and delegate: Time to figure out how to lose some of the day-to-day stress in your life so you can replenish.

6. Look for real men, not cartoon princes. Adjust your criteria while dating or you will waste both his time and yours.

(continued)

7. Add your own bits of glamour and excitement. Go in search of activities that up your drama quotient.

8. See the fantasy in hindsight. Instead of pining for a blank slate, determine what you want from a real man.

9. Go in search of new relationship models. Learn what you can from real-life couples who are making their relationship work.

10. Schedule the Mom talk. Ask your mother what she expected from her own love life, and see what you picked up from her.

11. Decide whether your current guy is a good fit. Take off the fantasy goggles and look at your boyfriend with clarity.

12. Tune in to your inner voice: Should you turn a new page or end the story?

13. In case of emergency: Set up a health team who can rescue you.

5

The Late Bloomer

Definition: You have been living your life on hold while waiting for your future husband.

Pop Quiz

You would take that exotic vacation you've been dreaming about, but:

- **A** You were hoping that it would be your honeymoon destination.
- **B** The economy is killing you—maybe next year.
- **C** You just took a solo adventure trip last month and need a break from vaccinations.

If you answered A, then this chapter is for you.

ZINA'S STORY

Zina,* 44, has been dreaming of buying her own place for years. After she "threw away" her money renting apartments for the past ten years, she wants to own. She dreams of being able to use nails to hang things instead of tape, paint her walls actual colors, and start investing in real art pieces. She has a great job and can afford to buy a place, espccially with the tax credit being offered to first-time home buyers.

The only thing standing in Zina's way is her worry that if she buys herself a place, it would be like unofficially giving up on marrying someone. According to Zina, "I think some part of me feels like if my life is too good and comfortable, I will never meet someone." Also, while she understands that buying a place doesn't mean she's tied to it forever, she "just can't seem to get past this fear that I'm ruining my chances for love—that I'll be too complete on my own."

Stage of Singlehood

You thought you'd be married by now and, frankly, you're sad and more than a little frustrated that you're not. You had a life plan, and it most definitely included finding a husband and starting a family. It's not terribly complicated, and many of the people you know have managed to accomplish it. So why did *you* end up checking "single" on your Facebook relationship status? What also stings is that you have let plenty of opportunities go by—travel, adventure, buying your own place—because you expected to do these things with your husband. Now you're starting to realize life could pass you by if you keep thinking that "real life" doesn't start until marriage. Still, if you make yourself too comfortable and happy, does it means you're giving up on finding Mr. Right? You don't like thinking of yourself as a quitter and you sure don't want to resign yourself to a life alone.

The Great News

Maybe your plan to be married with kids hasn't yet happened, and that's a bitter pill to swallow. But if you look at your life just slightly differently you will see that the world is about to open up for you. Once you decide you no longer want to live life on hold, you can begin adding in the many pleasures you've been missing out on. Have you wanted to buy your own place? Adopt a dog from a shelter? Bike through Vietnam? Whatever you have been postponing until Mr. Right comes along can go directly into your Outlook calendar, and this chapter will give you the necessary steps to get there. You don't need a gold band around your finger to make your life legit.

The true payoff of taking your life off hold is the freedom and exhilaration you will experience. The icing on the cake is that you actually have a better (not worse) chance of finding a husband when you learn how to take care of your own needs. As relationship expert and coauthor of *The Complete Idiot's Guide to Finding Mr. Right* Josie Brown confirmed, "Usually it's when you settle in your life that you find Mr. Right because your happiness radiates a sense of well-being . . . and that's attractive." Think about it. If you had the choice to be with a man who enjoys his day-to-day life or one who's been putting off fun and adventure until he meets "the one," who would *you* opt to be with? Most of us prefer to be with people who don't need us, but rather *choose* us, and who we choose right back.

SHIFT YOUR THINKING

Forget the future, what about *today*?

Liz, 33, finally bought a condo after years of thinking about it. It's not that she couldn't afford one (although her budget was admittedly modest), but that she had always thought she'd purchase her own place after meeting Mr. Right. In the meantime, she was throwing money down the drain on rent and feeling frustrated knowing it was a good market to buy in. Finally, she started condo hunting, bought herself a cute little place, and never looked back. "I realized I wasn't giving up on the dream of getting married and having kids, I was just buying my own place. It was an investment decision in the end, and a good one."

"I can't wait to own my own house when I get married," "After I have kids, I'm going to plan more whimsical experiences in my life," "When I get married, I'm going to learn to cook and throw incredible dinner parties" . . . many of the single women I interviewed were living their lives on hold in some fundamental way. They want their lives to be good but not so good that it means they have given up on finding the right guy. For some, it was intentional ("I don't want to do fill-in-the-blank until I'm married and can share it with my husband"); for others, it was more of a subconscious thought that they might be jinxing themselves out of a mate. The glaring problem is that in either case you are living your life with the volume turned way down.

When I asked many of the women I interviewed how their lives would change, something important happened: they realized for the first time that it wouldn't be tragic if they didn't marry.

They had been living with the fear that they might never marry, and had never really stopped to picture what it would—make that *could*—look like if they didn't. They had never considered it, and no one had ever asked them about it. Apparently, the idea of remaining single is so terrifying to some people that it is off-limits in conversation. Unfortunately, what that means is that single women are often living with an unnecessary anxiety that could be alleviated had they been able to talk through other options for their future.

Sure, most women I talked to got a disappointed expression on their faces when I first asked about the possibility of not marrying. But when I had them describe what their lives would look like, they brought up having close friends; indulging in hobbies they loved (cooking, gardening, going to museums, white-water rafting); working at jobs that excited them; making a difference by volunteering; dating (yes, they realized, there would still be men and sex in their lives); and traveling around the world. Some said they'd figure out a way to have kids (adopt, freeze their eggs, go through IVF), others said they wouldn't have children alone but spend time with kids (mentees, nieces, goddaughters, etc.).

Plenty of women looked relieved and even happy once they realized they could have a perfectly wonderful life whether they get hitched or not. "Wow," said one thirtysomething woman after our interview, "I just realized that it's the *not knowing* whether I'll find a husband that's so hard for me." Other women said they'd feel sad forgoing a husband and kids but knew they would set up a good life anyway. They just needed some steps to get things moving, which you will find below.

ACTION ITEMS

Let go of what you can't control.

First things first, remind yourself that you can't control when you might meet Mr. Right-for-You. You can stack the odds by putting yourself out there (you have a much better chance meeting a potential partner if you get yourself to a social event rather than watch *American Idol* at home in your sweatpants). You can be open to meeting someone, radiate positive energy, date online, and tell everyone you know that you're looking and open to blind dates. But at a certain point, meeting the right man for you is up to the fates.

The bad news is that you can't control something you care about deeply. This is hard for the many women who are used to being rewarded for their efforts. Paying your dues at the office often results in climbing the career ladder. Being smart with your money can lead to a better return on your investments. If you've worked at being a good friend, you're most likely going to be paid back by having good friends. There's logic to all of this. So it's frustrating that "putting yourself out there" in hopes of meeting a good guy doesn't necessarily result in finding him.

The good news is, if you can accept the fact that you can't control when you'll meet him, you are freed up to put that energy toward what you can control—like taking steps to make yourself happy. For some, it may mean scheduling something as grandiose as an architectural dig in Bora-Bora. For others, it may be as simple as checking out a new band downtown. What matters is that you take advantage of the opportunity to live well—right now.

Appreciate what's been there all along.

Women sometimes get so fixated on the idea of Mr. Right entering the picture that it's easy to forget that there are many other things that make them happy. I like how Garland Waller, a Boston University professor of TV and film, put it: "I think being alone, unless you choose it, is painful. I remember thinking, 'God, all I have is my family and my friends and my job and I'm so alone,' instead of 'Hey, I've got my family and my friends and my job—and this is a good life!'"

 ## Write it down: What in life do you take for granted?

Spend ten to fifteen minutes writing the answers in your journal. The list may include experiencing fits of laughter with friends; a career that makes you feel stimulated more often than not; being physically healthy so you can snowboard or try Pilates classes; having a pet that is ecstatic to see you at the end of the day; having a little time to crawl under your cozy covers on a frigid day; meeting a friend for a mocha Frappuccino; being connected to a larger community; whatever it is that makes your day sweeter.

One of two things will likely happen when you read your list. Either you're going to realize how much more wonderful your life is than you even realized, or you are going to see enough blank white space to make it clear that you need to make a point of creating more joy. Don't feel bad if there is too much white space; appreciate that you're at a starting place where life can only get fuller. This is a *beginning*.

Maybe it's been so long since you looked at what makes you

happy that you're not sure what does it for you anymore. In a blog post called "7 Questions to Finding Your True Passion" on INeedMotivation.com, blogger Frederic Premji suggests asking yourself, "Is there a particular event, a particular topic that makes your whole face just lighten up? Whatever it is that makes you smile, and makes you happy whenever you encounter it, this is a sign of something you are passionate about." Take note over the next few weeks of what makes you smile and why, and see if that can translate into a new activity to try.

 ## Tune in to your voice: What's missing for you right now?

Sit quietly and ask yourself what exactly is missing from your life. Perhaps the first thing that comes to mind is a man to share it with. There is nothing wrong with that. As Dr. Karen Gail Lewis, a marriage and family therapist, states: "Women want to be in relationships, we are relationship beings. We want to love, and we want to connect with others and be loved." There is nothing to apologize for. It becomes problematic only when it is the sole focus of your life, so much so that you can't appreciate the love and beauty that already surrounds you. The question isn't, "Is it okay to need a man in my life?" but rather, "What do I want my life to look like until he comes along—or *regardless* of whether he comes along."

Are your experiencing enough happiness? Is there excitement? Are you being mentally challenged? Is there a void on your list of life's pleasures that you always wanted to try: living abroad, buying a house, adopting a pet, learning to cook, or even something as simple as buying season's tickets to a sporting event or the theater. Maybe you've put off tennis lessons because it's something you always pictured doing with your future husband. Or joining a gourmet club with a bunch of new people. Or booking a cruise during your next vacation. Or learning to paint in watercolor.

 ## Write it down: What are you putting off until you're married?

Spend ten to fifteen minutes jotting down in your journal the changes you would make to your life and things you would like to try. When you are done, look at your list. Circle the items that you could do this year. Put a star next to the items you could do this month. Then put at least one of those items on your calendar—and do it.

Maybe reality says your paycheck doesn't cover a ten-day trip to Costa Rica or a scuba-diving adventure this year; see if there is a short-term alternative that can start feeding the passion. Thuy, mentioned in the opening story of chapter 6, loves traveling at least once or twice a year but needed something to give her the same joie de vivre when she wasn't overseas. Recently she joined a guitar society in her hometown, with each member hosting a guitar party in their home on their designated night. She also signed up for a local mushroom foraging class through her local adult-ed program. "I know it sounds dorky," she said laughing, "but mushrooms are really cool!"

Wendy, 40, has a book club where she and her girlfriends read books set in or involving other countries; whoever is hosting cooks a typical meal from that country and everyone else brings snacks or dessert. Their favorite session was for the book *Eat, Pray, Love,* when they feasted on authentic Italian pasta and wine and talked about their own life adventures.

If your purchase is big—a car, a house, moving across the country—and you can afford it, allow yourself the permission. Nobody is going to say, "Hey, lady, you are ready now, so go ahead and take the plunge." That has to come from you. (Note: If you can afford it but don't believe you deserve to be happy, then working through that issue becomes top priority; if it's too big to take on yourself, find a therapist to guide you.) There shall be no more limiting yourself for no good reason. Additionally, remind yourself that living fully now doesn't keep you from finding someone. Learning how to make yourself happy—and the confidence that brings—makes you *more* attractive to a man. Who doesn't want to hang out with someone who appreciates his or her own worth?

Josie, the relationship editor mentioned previously, added, "Women have in their mind the idea of the white picket fence with a man carrying the woman over the threshold. How you get over that threshold is not what's important. Having a place, a home that makes you feel happy, is what's important. Also, who says buying your own place has anything to do with finding Mr. Right? He may sell you your house, he may fix your house, or he may be your new neighbor!"

You can replace the word "house" here for whatever it is that you've been postponing. Knowing what makes you fulfilled—and figuring out how to get it on your own, even when it's a real challenge—is a prerequisite to any version of happily ever after. This ability to meet your own needs (even just *knowing* your own needs) is something sacred that no one can take away from you once you have it. Also, no husband can do this for you, so you'd better figure it out for yourself now.

Create your potential future in a scrapbook.

Little girls who dream of weddings sometimes make scrapbooks of their big day. I like the scrapbook twist that Jerusha Stewart, author of *The Last Single Girl in the World*, came up with. She told me that she too once held the fear that she'd never get married and would end up lost and alone. And then one day Jerusha forced herself to figure out what her life would actually be like if she did remain single. Would it be a life of resentment and heartache or might it look like something else? She decided to examine this by making a scrapbook of what her life *could* look like if she stayed solo.

She sat down with a bunch of magazines and cut out photos of her possible future. She snipped pictures of travel vacations, hanging with girlfriends over coffee, going on dates with handsome, interesting men and all sorts of other possibilities. By the time she pasted the pictures in and flipped through the pages, she felt better, even happy. Having a husband wasn't the be-all and end-all. What she saw before her was a life of possibility and enjoyment. "Sometimes, we fear things because we can't picture them," she said, "so this was a perfect way to eliminate the fear and start living."

Why not try this yourself? You can do it by yourself and keep adding to the scrapbook as you find more images that please you; or you can invite over a bunch of girlfriends and make it a group event. Add a pitcher of mimosa, put on some great music, and call it a "reinvent your future" brunch. B.Y.O.S. (bring your own scrapbook).

 ## Write it down: How can you get the ball rolling?

Maybe you're thinking, "I want to go for it, really I do, but I'm just not ready!" That's okay. Focus on taking steps to get things moving. Start by asking yourself:

- How much money will I need once I'm ready?
- Are there other resources I'll need?
- Are there things I'll need to do to prepare?
- Can I talk to others who have achieved this goal, and learn more about their experience?
- What will it take in order for me to be ready when the time is right?

Take notes in your journals and make to-do lists, and consider it the first step toward realizing your dreams. It may even be helpful to create self-imposed deadlines, such as "Call expert by end of this month to find out costs" or "Research three options on the Internet by next Monday." The idea is to break down your goals into manageable tasks.

Claudine, for instance, has been thinking about throwing a bash for herself. She said she used to joke about how great it would be if there was something akin to a wedding reception, a big party for moving to your own place. "I remember mentioning that to a friend," she said, "who said, 'Yeah, it's called a housewarming party,' and I thought, 'No, it doesn't have the same meaning. It is more of a I'm-a-grown-up-now bash.'" Claudine isn't ready to plan the party quite yet, but she's mulling over ideas and building her confidence.

Maxi,* 46, wants to go back to grad school and get a degree in art history. "I majored in business because my parents convinced me that it was impractical to study art," she said. "I really regret listening to them because one of my greatest pleasures is walking through art galleries and museums and I wish I had the knowledge to really know the works and compare them. So I'm saving my money to be able to go back to school and do this. It's going to take a while but I just know it's something I need to do for myself. I'm setting aside a little money each month and looking into all kinds of financial assistance."

If money is your main obstacle (real or perceived), make a monthly budget (Google "Monthly Budget Template" and take your pick). You'll need to know what you realistically can afford to spend as you're considering your options. Taking your life off hold should not break the bank or leave you in debt. Also, don't despair if you can't afford that trip to Asia or scuba-diving lessons in Maui; there are always ways to scale down and live large. For instance, take an Asian cooking class and host a dinner party when you graduate; or sign up for scuba-diving lessons locally and save for your first adventure abroad. What's important is to start focusing on what makes you feel alive and then pursuing those things.

Appreciate your adventures— even when they tank.

You may have a clear vision of what your new adventures will be like—only to find out that they end up looking nothing like it. They may even bomb. Having bumps along the way is part of the journey. Life coach Bob Proctor said, "It is important to acknowledge a mistake instantly, correct it, and learn from it. That literally turns a failure into a success. Success is on the far side of failure." So instead of getting frazzled and disheartened, see your blunders as life lessons (although every once in a while they are just plain bummers, and that's part of some journeys too).

Robin, 33, a world traveler, said, "I still remember my first road trip alone. One of my friends canceled just before we were supposed to leave, and I went anyway. I remember I kept driving around the hotel thinking 'Oh my gosh, I can't go in myself. What are they going to think of me,' and just freaking out. But eventually, I had to get sleep, so I parked the car and did it." After that hurdle, which ended up being no big deal, Robin began traveling alone on a regular basis, which she says makes her feel powerful. When she faces challenging moments, like "getting overcharged by a taxi driver in Rome because I can't speak Italian," she "learns from it and moves on." She wastes no time berating herself or feeling ashamed.

You, like Robin, will have to deal with plenty of imperfections when you take risks. So what? You're experiencing adventure and learning how to navigate new situations and pick up new life skills. Say to yourself something along the lines of "Good for you for taking a risk. That wasn't easy and you did it anyway! It took guts." Then congratulate yourself for the parts that go well

("Nice pick on the hotel!"); go easy on yourself when things fall apart ("So what if I got a flat tire?"); and appreciate when you get yourself through tricky moments ("Way to go using your iPhone to find the local towing service so you can get back on the road tomorrow"). Ending up back on your feet is the point, along with appreciating the journeys you brave.

Open the door when opportunity knocks.

There are plenty of times when new opportunities will come to you, even when you're not sure you're ready or you don't like the opportunity presented. There you are minding your own business, when opportunity knocks its loud, annoying knock and you have to open the door. It's either that or wonder what the knocking was all about. Instead of getting flustered by this unwanted opportunity, see if there's something that makes the situation worthwhile.

Daisy, 35, for instance, hadn't intended to live alone. But after she and her live-in boyfriend broke up fairly suddenly, she had to find a new place to live quickly. "It was scary because I didn't know if I could do it financially or emotionally, I just didn't know if I was capable. But I did it anyway, and by the end of that summer, I was going out with my friends, dancing, enjoying dinners, seeing events around town, and it was great. I would come home at night and read magazines and have a cup of tea and not worry about keeping anyone awake. I'm a night owl, and now I can stay up and read until two in the morning and it doesn't bother anybody."

Kathy,* 43, got laid off when the economy started going south. She had been a real estate agent and hated it but was too afraid to quit because she'd gotten good at it and it was paying the bills. Her life, she said, was "good enough." In her head, she'd planned to become an event planner once she got married and there was a partner bringing in a salary to fall back on. But two days after getting laid off, she saw an ad on Craigslist for a woman who was looking for a partner to do event planning with. The two met, talked for hours, and Kathy signed on for the role. "It was terrifying," Kathy admits. "I knew very little about how to plan events. But my partner has ended up being a mentor to me, teaching me the ropes. I can't believe I postponed it for so long."

 ## Tune in to your inner voice: What freaks you out about this opportunity?

If you're excited by an opportunity but also anxious, take a minute to close your eyes and ask yourself what's making you feel that way. Is there something about the opportunity that feels inherently wrong, or is it the fact that you weren't planning on its showing up this minute? How do you feel when you imagine going for it? Are there any logical reasons to pass on this experience?

Sometimes taking your life off hold means being brave enough to try something you are pretty sure is right for you—even if you're not 100 percent ready. Assure yourself that you're not nearly as fragile as you sometimes suspect. If it goes badly, you'll find your way out and learn what to do differently next time. Or maybe upon close consideration, you'll realize that the timing around this opportunity is so bad that "going for it" at this moment would tank any chance of success. That's, of course, a valid reason to pass. Instead of feeling depressed about it, think through what requirements you will need to set in place moving forward and what you can do to get closer to meeting those requirements. What matters most is that you don't cast off possibilities because you get scared; you want to think through each one so you can make decisions with intention.

Schedule the Mom talk: Tell her you're taking your life off hold.

When Suzanna, 35, decided to buy her own house, she called her mother to celebrate. After all, she had earned enough money to make a down payment on her own house—what a victory! Instead, her mom was silent for a few moments and then said, "I guess you're giving up on marriage, huh?" Suzanna, who had been overjoyed two minutes earlier, cursed herself for thinking her mom might say something positive. "She's so desperate for me to get married that she couldn't even appreciate what a huge achievement it was. She never would have been able to buy her own house when she was my age."

Like Suzanna, a lot of women have to deal with mothers who insist their daughters keep the eyes on the prize (a husband) every second. Surprisingly, even moms who spent their twenties and thirties fighting for women's rights often worry about their daughters being too independent. Yes, this is a problem. But it's essential to start making it your *mom's* problem—and not yours— if she's going to continue to question your lifestyle choices.

Tell her, "You know, Mom, you're going to notice some major changes I'm making in my life. For a long time I haven't taken big risks or made major investments because I was waiting for

Mr. Right. I'm not waiting anymore; if he comes, he comes. I hope you'll be happy for me because this is a huge step." If she needs guidance, tell her exactly what you want her to say to you so she can't mess up, such as: "I would love it if when I tell you about something new I'm trying, you'd say, 'Good for you!' or 'I can't wait to hear about it!'"

You may have to nudge her back on track sometimes. If you tell her, for example, you're saving up for your own place and she responds, "But what if you buy a place of your own and then meet someone?" you can smile and say, "I think what you meant to say is, 'Good for you.'" This is not to be delivered with a passive-aggressive tone, just straight up. She will catch on—even if it takes her half a dozen times.

Become the role model you never had.

As mentioned, one of the things that make it so difficult to picture a happy life if you are single in your thirties is that few of us grew up seeing any positive role models for what it could look like. Think about how much easier all of this might have been if you had a single woman in your childhood telling you about her fabulous life.

Certainly the majority of women I interviewed grew up with the belief that if you were single past thirty, your life was pretty much done for. It was sad, even pathetic. They knew divorced parents, and that's what single life looked like. But the few women I spoke to who actually had positive single role models—a cool aunt, a passionate teacher, an adventurous neighbor—had a much more optimistic view about living a life unmarried.

Debbie, 43, recalled, "My aunt Titi was a wild woman. She was single in her thirties and she just didn't care about getting married. During the day, she had a corporate job that must have paid pretty well, although I can't remember what it was. And then at night, she'd paint the town red. It was the '70s and she would wear tight jeans and high boots and funky hats and go out dancing on weekends, and traveling to Europe sometimes. I thought she was fabulous, and I wanted to be just like her. When she let me try on her high heels or purple jackets, I was just the happiest. She showed me that you don't have to be professional *or* fun, that you could really combine the two and whatever else you were interested in."

Micah,* 38, said she had a college professor who showed her how great it could be to be a single woman. "At college I had this professor who was a single woman, the only one I knew that old. She was probably in her late forties. She taught archaeology and she would go on annual digs and she had these amazing photos of her all around the world, and I just thought she was the sexiest, most interesting woman I'd ever met. It totally undid my view that being single meant you were home watching bad TV with cats milling around your feet. It meant flying off to Greece for a dig and making a difference in the world. Looking back, I'm sure she had her share of lonely moments or worries about growing old alone, but I didn't get that vibe from her. She seemed just really excited about life."

Something you can do for the next generation of girls while boosting your own confidence is to share your courageous new journey with the girls in your life and tell them about the steps you are taking. If they see you making a truly interesting life for yourself without a husband, you open their eyes to possibilities beyond the pages of their princess books.

Laurie, 31, said she loves showcasing that being single isn't a limitation: "I enjoy whenever someone says, 'I could never do that!' as in, 'I could never go to movies alone or fly across the country for one night to see my favorite band alone.' I feel strong, like a pioneer!"

You don't have to be happy 100 percent of the time around the girls you spend time with, or convince them that being single is the best choice. Just allowing others to see that you're not waiting for the prince to show up will open their minds about what happiness can look like. It will also reinforce for *you* how far you have come in taking your life off hold.

 ## In case of emergency: Track your efforts, boost your courage.

After you accomplish a new goal, no matter how big or small, write in your journal what the experience felt like so you have somewhere to turn when you need your next shot of motivation. Record how it felt setting out to accomplish your goal; what the process was like, and how you felt when you completed it. What did you learn? What would you do differently next time? If you didn't achieve the goal, record what got in your way and what you will do in the future to fix that. Consider this book a confidence booster to rely upon when you're about to head out of your comfort zone. Read through it, and take stock of the fact that you've been in this uncomfortable place plenty of times before and ended up just fine—or even better.

$ DON'T BUST YOUR SAVINGS ACCOUNT IF YOU TRAVEL

If you are planning a vacation, it may be tempting to spare no expense. The idea is that you deserve to spoil yourself after so many years of not spending money on yourself. You do, but you don't want to come back strapped for cash and worried about paying your bills. Plan ahead exactly how much money you can afford to spend on your trip, and don't go over it. Before you leave for your destination: Find special rates and deals for day trips; pay for taxis to special places you want to go rather than tour groups (which bleed you dry); and vow to yourself that you won't go beyond your means when it comes to buying souvenirs. While you're there, enjoy picnic lunches at local hot spots and bring snacks with you so you won't spend your cash dining in tourist traps.

5 KEY TIPS FOR SAFE SOLO TRAVEL

If your inner travel bug is screaming yes! but your inner worrywart is shouting no! book your ticket and take comfort in the safety travel tips below. (For more pointers, check out *Fly Solo: The 50 Best Places on Earth for a Girl to Travel Alone* by Teresa Rodriguez Williamson, a great practical guide for newbie travelers.)

(continued)

1. Bring a small handbag (rather than a large pocketbook) that you can keep close to your body so no one can snatch it from you.
2. Leave the jewels at home. In fact, carry the minimal amount of valuables with you on a trip.
3. If you do get lost (happens to the best of us), be aware of your surroundings and act like you know where you are going until you get to a safe place to ask directions.
4. Pass on low necklines. You don't have to dress like a hausfrau, but stay away from miniskirts and supertight clothing so you don't attract unwanted (and possibly harmful) attention.
5. Write down the name, address, and phone number of your hotel and keep it in your pocket when you go out (one strong local cocktail can make you forget your own name).

 ## REMINDER CHECKLIST

1. Let go of what you can't control. Say buh-bye to the things that you have no say over.
2. Appreciate what's been there all along. Take a step back and feel joy for all that you have in your life.
3. Write it down: What positive things in your life do you sometimes take for granted?
4. Tune in to your voice: What's missing for you right now?
5. Write it down: What are you putting off until you're married?
6. Create your potential future in a scrapbook. Envision for yourself a happy life if you don't marry.

7. Write it down: How can you get the ball rolling?

8. Appreciate your adventures—even when they tank. Take away lessons from a risk that misfires.

9. Open the door when opportunity knocks. Get used to assessing possibilities even when you didn't plan for them.

10. Tune in to your inner voice: What freaks you out about this opportunity?

11. Schedule the mom talk. Explain to mom that you are making major lifestyle changes but aren't throwing in the towel on the idea of marriage.

12. Become the role model you never had. By showing others you are living a full life, you'll be reminded of your successes.

13. In case of emergency: Track your efforts, boost your courage.

6

The Committed Free Spirit

Definition: You worry that having independence and a committed relationship is like trying to have your cake and eat it too.

Pop Quiz

If you won a ticket to a Broadway show tonight, you would:

(A) Sell it last-minute on Craigslist; no way are you going alone.
(B) Try to cajole a friend into buying a ticket and coming along.
(C) Make a night of it by taking yourself out to dinner first.

If you answered C, this chapter is for you.

THUY'S STORY

Thuy, a 31-year-old attorney, told me when I first met her that she wanted to find a man to share her life with, but she was in no rush. In fact, she says her love of adventure really started after her last boyfriend dumped her. It was just before they were supposed to go on an international trip together. Her first reaction was to hit the carton of Häagen-Dazs and bawl her eyes out. But after the tears dried, she had an inspiring idea: Why not go somewhere glamorous on her own?

She booked a trip to Italy—and had the time of her life. "Yes, there were some concessions I had to make," Thuy said, "like not going out late at night alone and fending off some offers from foreign men, but the experience was amazing! I loved it." Now Thuy travels by herself somewhere exotic every year: trekking through Thailand, Morocco, and Guatemala. Here's the problem: She started seeing a man in his late thirties who is ready to settle down with her—and join her on her exotic international vacations. "I love him," Thuy said, "but I don't want to lose the free-spirit side of me. It's also hard because there's all this pressure to settle down."

Stage of Singlehood

Ten years ago, you would have put money on the fact that you'd be cooking family dinners and driving your kids to soccer games in a minivan. But it didn't work out that way, for whatever reason. The natural reaction for many would be disappointment and frustration, but you're not feeling either. The truth is, you love the freedom that comes from making your own decisions and calling the shots. Who needs a gas-guzzling minivan? You sometimes hear wedding bells in the distant future, but right now the call of independence rings louder. In fact, you crave alone time so frequently you wonder if you're cut out for commitment. But you do still want to marry. If only you could have both. Is this normal, or are you trying to have your cake and eat it too?

The Great News

For once, you *get* to have your cake and eat it too. You don't have to choose between a close, intimate relationship with a man and the independent streak you now pride yourself on. The key is to find a guy who celebrates your indie ways and is grateful for your lack of neediness. As long as you're willing to work on finding the right balance as a couple, there's no need to cancel those one-person adventures and nights out with the girls. Hopefully, you've got the right guy beside you, and just need some practical strategies to help maintain the balance of solo and together time.

If you're not sure whether your boyfriend is the right guy for you, there is still good news. You may find he's more on board with your need for space than you think; he's just confused and needs help understanding that your desire for "me time" is not a reflection of your desire for him. Or maybe your need for space is relatively new—and both of you are adjusting to this recent shift. That's fine, every couple goes through growth periods where someone's needs change and the other requires a little time to catch up. If, on the other hand, you discover that your boyfriend is the wrong partner for you—and it becomes crystal clear he's not going to accept your independent side—then the writing is on the wall. You will need to let him go so you can find a guy who accepts you without resentment. It may not sound like great news that you're facing a potential breakup, but it is in the long run, because it means you're not going to compromise a major part of your core self for another person.

SHIFT YOUR THINKING

Relationships don't have one look.

Many women grew up thinking that committed couples have a specific look—namely, they do everything together. They cook dinner together and go to shows and take walks in the park and have deep discussions over morning coffee and are joined at the hip. You fantasized about creating a world enmeshed, two becoming one. What you didn't predict was that you would end up spending a whole bunch of years creating an independent life for yourself—and not wanting to let go of it.

After all, you've had plenty of time to taste the thrill of making major decisions by yourself without checking in with anyone. You've probably got a strong support group of girlfriends, and either found a career path for yourself or you are exploring a new one after getting real-life experience under your belt. You've also felt the pleasures of exploring different sides of yourself that you didn't even know existed. Maybe you've found your inner travel bug (like Thuy in the opening story), discovered a new hobby or interest you never could have expected, and love parading around your place doing whatever you like when you want to. The idea of being entwined with someone now makes you feel squirmy, not swoony.

"I need a lot of alone time," said Mira,* 29. "This wasn't always the case. I grew up in a house full of brothers and sisters and loved it, thought I'd want a big family with someone. But when I moved out and tasted life on my own, I loved every aspect of it once I got used to it. I liked the quiet, cooking for myself, watching whatever I want on TV. I finally get to be selfish." About a year ago, Mira started dating her boyfriend and, although she cares about him, she worries that he sometimes resents her need for so much time apart from him. "I don't want to break up with him," she says, "but if he can't deal with me needing my own space, we're going to have issues. Am I being selfish, and is this okay?"

Yes. In fact, it's more than okay to be selfish (not self-absorbed but concerned about taking care of yourself). Needing time on your own is not something you can (or should be asked to) change about yourself. It's part of your makeup, just as much as your height, foot size, or the sound of your laugh. It means you have the confidence and inner fortitude to get by on your own while enjoying the experience. But it does also mean that if you want to be in a long-term relationship, you're probably going to need to find a partner who values alone time as well, and you will have to work on making your time together more meaningful because it's limited. Also, be prepared to compromise (being independent isn't synonymous with always getting your way), and find a man who is equally willing to negotiate how much time he demands of you. This chapter is all about giving you the tools to make sure you have ways to keep your independence and relationship commitment in harmony.

ACTION ITEMS

 Tune in to your inner voice:
Is commitment in the cards for you?

Spend a few quiet minutes asking yourself whether you truly *want* to commit to someone, or whether you're with your guy because you don't feel like dealing with the hassle of breaking up. Or maybe you've been seduced by the fact that everyone else in your life is so happy that you found a nice guy and are avoiding the heartache of telling everyone it's kaput. In your heart of hearts you know that it's not okay to stay with your man just because it seems like too much work and emotional effort to break up, but it never seems that it's the right time or that you're in the right place to end things.

Grace, 36, realized the hard way that she wasn't up for commitment. She was engaged to two different men (before age thirty) and ended both relationships. It was only during her second engagement that she finally understood that she wasn't ready to settle down and create a family. But unfortunately, Grace didn't listen to that voice inside her head, and ended up cheating on her fiancé two months before the wedding. "He was a really wonderful guy who knew he wanted to get married and settle down. I didn't, but I couldn't figure out how to get out of it, and I'm sorry for what I did because I don't think it was fair." Luckily, she says, he went on to marry another woman and "I'm in a much better place now too." In fact, the last time I talked to Grace, she was happy to report she had a baby with her latest boyfriend but still had no interested in marriage. They're figuring out their own path.

If your inner voice says you are not ready for a committed relationship, in spite of your age and expectations from those around you, follow that voice. It is telling you a truth. Rather than drag things out with your guy, consider ending things sooner rather than later. If you can't hear any inner voice, try again later—it comes with practice. Continue making time to sit quietly by yourself or go for a walk, and see if anything changes over the next month when you tune in. If your inner voice reports back that you *are* ready to commit but this is not the right person, accept that too. It is what it is.

Assess whether your guy is on board with your schedule.

Only you know whether your boyfriend is a good match for you. But one thing is for certain: Assuming you're a woman who strongly values her independence, you'll need a man who loves strong women. He may be annoyed by your need for space sometimes, like when he wants you to join him for a company dinner and you have plans to go backpacking with a friend, but overall he should appreciate that you're a woman who can see to her own needs and who enjoys life.

After her last breakup, Rachel, 37, realized that she was going to have to find someone unconventional like herself if she was going to have a successful relationship with a guy. "We women really start our lives at thirty these days and sometimes get our career together first instead of starting a family. I know a couple of people who married young and are still married and have 2.2 kids and lead a more conventional life than me. I am a writer and I travel around the world and I'm not the type of person who can get up and take the bus to work and go to a corporation and then get home at five and pick my kid up at day care." Rachel knows that if she's going to be with someone, he's going to have to be a nontraditional guy who fits into her lifestyle or a conventional guy who loves that she is a free spirit and won't try to change her.

Daisy, 33, realized things weren't going to work out with her boyfriend after he kept making it clear that he resented her need to spend so much time with her girlfriends: "I think he wanted it to be a little simpler; he was always asking why there were all these other people in my life. We had nights where it was just the two of us, but I have a lot of friends, and my work requires me to be really social. And I like it; I like being out." She went on to say that while she likes having couple time, she also wants to have plenty to talk about with her boyfriend about what they did separately. Ultimately, it became too big of an issue and they broke up. Going forward, Daisy knows to look for a man who also has a life of his own and is not looking to become "one" with another person.

Maybe your guy, like Daisy's, is not a good fit for you because he has a dissimilar vision of a relationship. It's not right or wrong, it's just different from your own. It's highly possible, however, that he is right for you but you just haven't come up with a way to find the right balance and communicate your needs for time with each other. If that's the case, you need a plan that sits right for both of you and can be tweaked along the way. Coming up with this plan—and following through—definitely takes effort, dedication, and the desire to keep things on the right path as a couple, but it's what will keep you connected to each other.

 ## Write it down: What does a healthy relationship look like to you?

It's one thing to tell your guy, "I'm going to need space in this relationship," or "You need to appreciate that I'm an independent person." But what does that mean? What does it look like? It's time to create an indie blueprint—a basic sketch of what will, and won't, work for you in a relationship. Spend twenty to thirty minutes writing down answers in your journal to the following questions (with the understanding that your answers may change, but this is how you feel right now):

- What, if anything, makes you feel anxious about spending too much time together?
- Why is it important to you to have plenty of alone time?
- How many days or nights in any given week would you like to spend time with your guy?
- Would you prefer to go on trips and adventures with him, or by yourself (or with your girlfriends)?
- How would you describe a healthy balance of independence and couple time?

Singles coach Trisha Stone says in her article "Dating/ Relationships & Independence" on SelfGrowth.com: "What you must become clear about is what elements of your independent life you want to retain. Think about the must-haves. These may be things like time, certain kinds of space, and a certain amount of time to spend with friends and family."

Of course, you're not the only one in your relationship and you're going to have to talk through with your boyfriend how much time you'll spend together and what that time will look like. But in order to negotiate with him you need to start from a place of understanding of what works for you and where you can compromise. That is where a blueprint, based on your answers to the questions above, comes in handy.

Your indie blueprint might look something like this:

I feel anxious that he is going to want to become one of those couples who are joined at the hip like other people I know. That's just not me, it makes me feel claustrophobic. I need to be my own person who can still act on a whim at times. If I had my druthers, I'd spend three or four nights a week with him but not more than that. I am not ready to fully combine our lives yet. Maybe I will be, but I'm not right now. A healthy relationship would like us picking three nights a week that we know are ours together, whether we have a plan or are just hanging out. The other nights are reserved for me to take care of my apartment, hang out with my pets, spend time with my friends, and take care of myself.

Share your blueprint with your man.

It's easy to assume that your guy will take your independence in stride and assume that you're both on the same page. You may be thinking, "Part of the reason that he likes me so much is because I am not needy. So I'm sure he's fine with me making my own plans for myself," or "If he had a problem with my going out without him, he'd tell me, right?" Not necessarily. Your guy might have hoped that your independent streak would mellow once you committed to each other. He may be worried that he likes you more than you like him (we tend to resort back to junior high insecurities in these vulnerable moments) because you're always running off to do something by yourself while he stays home alone. Or, yes, it's possible that he is thrilled with your need to do things alone and he brags about it to all his guy friends. The point is, you have no idea until you talk to him. Furthermore, if you want this to be a lasting relationship, you need to communicate what it is that you want and find out whether he wants the same thing.

"I know that I need to spend a lot of time with my friends," says Frankie,* 27. "We are a really tight support network. My boyfriend understands this and is cool with it. At one point in our relationship, however, he told me that he wasn't getting enough time with me because I was always out with my friends. I told him he was invited to come out with us, but he said that is not the same as having one-on-one time. He wanted my undivided attention when we were together. So I scaled back and started scheduling at least three nights a week with him, and it's going well. At first I thought he was being a little demanding, but I started to see that he needed to feel valued. My boyfriend and I still have to work out what's enough time together, but we're getting better at it and that feels good."

Sit down with your guy when he has a quiet moment and tell him you're checking in about your time together. Do not ask, "Can we talk about our relationship later tonight?" which will make him crazy and leave him assuming you're ending things. By the time you sit down together, he will be in such a state of anxiety that it doesn't matter what you say, the conversation will veer south. Instead, choose a time when you already know he is free and tell him specifically that you want to make sure you're both on track in terms of whether you're spending a good amount of time together. Let him know whether you're getting enough time to yourself, whether you're feeling like you have to defend your need for time alone, and what changes, if any, you'd like to see moving forward. Don't blame him or accuse him of needing too much; use the opportunity to make your needs heard. Yelling "You don't give me any space!" is only going to make him shut down emotionally.

One mistake we women tend to make with men is assuming we should go into deep and soulful talks that are filled with details and examples. Good communication with your guy will look different than it does with your girlfriends. In her book *You Just Don't Understand*, Deborah Tannen states, "Women must learn that the kind of intimate talk they have with their girlfriends should remain just that. Trying to turn your man into a girlfriend will usually fail because men, in general, don't create feelings of closeness in that way." The good news is that men are known for taking the problem-solving route, and you are checking in with him about whether there is any problem to fix.

Ask him how *he* feels about the quantity of your time spent together, whether it is enough for him or not, and what his needs are. Listen and ask questions if you need clarification (such as, "So you're happy with how things are now?" or "Do you wish we spent more time together?"). Hopefully, the conversation will run smooth and you'll be on the same page. If, however, he starts accusing you of spending too much time away from the roost, tell him this is exactly why you wanted to have this conversation, to better understand each other's needs. Stay focused on what is working for you both now, and what changes are acceptable going forward. You should both be willing to compromise—so long as it is not at the expense of your or his happiness.

It's time to change your Outlook (calendar).

Now is the time to put your new practices into play. On an Outlook or Google calendar you share (of course, you can always go retro with paper), mark the days of the month that will be devoted to couple time. Treat these days as sacrosanct and you will avoid all of the hassles of double booking and overexplaining your schedule to your guy. This will also allow your boyfriend (or you) to buy concert tickets, look into last-minute travel bargains, and have enough lead time to plan dating events in advance. By scheduling your nights together regularly, you assure him that you are making this relationship a priority, and vice versa.

This won't always work out perfectly. You'll find out last minute that on your scheduled night together your favorite author is reading at a bookstore around the corner—and your guy can't stand this type of writing. Or your best friend will call in tears because she got laid off from her job and needs a shoulder to cry on. Obviously there is a big difference between wanting to go hear an author and being there for your best friend when she needs you. You'll have to work out these calendar glitches as they arise, just as he will. But if you can stick to your dating schedule *overall*, you should be in good shape.

The other thing that's important is to make sure that when you do plan your time together, you're 100 percent there—and not thinking about other things you'd like to be doing or plans you're going to make for the next week. As Debbi Strange says in her article "How to Spend Quality Time with Your Boyfriend or Girlfriend," "Whether you and your mate live together or live separately makes no difference; you still need to find the time to have fun together and enjoy each other without feeling as though you are in a rush and need to be doing something else."

Amy,* 41, admits, "My boyfriend and I have a date night twice a week. It's our time to really connect and talk about the week and what's been going on in the outside world. What used to happen is my phone would be ringing off the hook with girlfriends who wanted to talk or who would text me, and my boyfriend would get totally aggravated. But I didn't want to leave my friends hanging. Eventually I realized that I needed to be present with whoever I was with and not worrying about anyone else. So I began turning off the ringer during date night and that helped a lot. That time together is about us and everything else and everybody else will have to wait."

If time spent together is already a sensitive issue for you and your boyfriend, then it's all the more important that you disconnect and unplug during your dates. If you can't resist the urge to peek at your iPhone to see who is calling or to send a quick text back to your friend, leave your gadgets at home. We forget how important it is to lock eyes on our partner and really pay attention to what they're saying. Get rid of the ringing, vibrating, beeping machines in your life for the night. Of course, you should expect the same from him.

Don't let others dictate your schedule.

If you are someone who needs plenty of time to yourself and your boyfriend doesn't mind at all, lovely. Don't take it personally when others get curious about whether your boyfriend's feelings are hurt or whether they think you're being selfish by not prioritizing your relationship. What's important is that the relationship works for both of you and whether you are both happy with the terms. Other people can worry about their own relationships.

One fortysomething woman told me, "I travel a lot for business, and so does my boyfriend, which means it's often a struggle to get us together in the same room. But we have a blast together, he's a wonderful, supportive guy, and I'm not looking to get married anytime soon, so this works for me. The problem is, I get constant flak from other people in my life who tell me I'm not making my relationship enough of a priority, or they criticize my boyfriend and me for not being more serious. The whole thing gets old, but during my insecure moments, I wonder if they're right, if I should be doing things differently."

You have to do what makes sense for you. Nobody can tell you exactly how much time you should be spending together or where you should be in your relationship. That's for you and your guy to determine. Once you feel comfortable with the ground rules you both have set up, you will feel confident saying to others, "It's all good. We have a system that is good for us," or "We may be a little untraditional, but we know what works for us." Let's face it: when we are clear about what we want, we are far less bothered by the no-holds-barred observations of others.

Lastly, check in with your inner voice regularly to make sure you're getting enough space—that your relationship feels solid and you're honoring your independence. Which one you crave more will likely depend on the week, what is going on in your life, and what opportunities pop up at any given time. As long as you remember to stay clear on what feels right for you—and make sure your partner is in the loop and feels respected—you can indulge in having your cake and eating it too.

Schedule the Mom talk: Ask her to think outside the relationship box.

So your mother wants to know how things are progressing in the relationship department. Or maybe she makes comments about her friends' children marrying or drops hints that she's ready to become a grandmother. She's forever asking what your boyfriend's intentions are and whether you're planning to settle down. One thing is for certain: If she doesn't stop talking to you about your relationship, you're going to throttle her.

Tell her that there's so much going on in your life, outside of your relationship, that you'd love to talk to her about. Give her an example ("Let me tell you about this idea I came up with at work," or "I met a new friend last week who is doing something really interesting"). This way, you're teaching her what you want to focus on.

Another suggestion to veer her away from relationship talk is to open up new topics of conversation with her. Ask her who one of her biggest inspirations has been, or what she dreamt about when she was a girl, or what she considers her biggest success. So often we see our mothers as "moms" and not as individual people with their own stories and experiences. In addition to sidetracking your mother off your love life, you can get to know each other better as women and understand what makes each other tick.

If she keeps harping on the state of your relationships and won't give up, you can take things a step farther by saying something like, "You know, Mom, it makes me sad that this is all you want to talk about with me. There is so much more to my life than my boyfriend. The truth is, when you keep at it like this, it makes me feel like you don't value me very much." She may not be thrilled, but you can bet you're going to get her attention—and will likely start seeing real changes. Repeat as necessary.

In case of emergency: Take a note to self.

If you are worried that being in a committed relationship is going to mean that you risk losing important parts of yourself, make sure that this doesn't happen. Take time to jot down a few of the most important qualities you worry will disappear—maybe your love for trying new things on your own, or taking risks, or making sure that you can fend for yourself. Also write down some of the solo opportunities you want to reserve for yourself so you won't forget. Check this list when you're feeling like your independence is being threatened. Are you staying true to yourself? Are you meeting your needs? If you're not, make a point of getting activities on the calendar that will get you back on track.

 ## BLEND, BUT DON'T MERGE

One way to retain your independence is to keep your own savings account rather than opening a joint account with your boyfriend. The problem with a joint account is that you are held equally liable if your boyfriend bounces a check or gets into deeper trouble. Of course, having your own bank account also means that you don't have to explain or defend your purchases to him. It should be noted that plenty of couples open up a joint account only to be used for household items and mutual expenses. That's fine, but if you are somebody who really doesn't want to answer to anyone about your purchases—and you are making responsible choices and paying for things with your own money—then stick with a solo account and each of you can pitch in to cover shared costs.

5 CLUES YOU'RE NOT READY TO COMMIT TO YOUR MAN

1. When your man gives you an engagement ring, your first thought is, "I wonder how much I can get for this on eBay."
2. You buy your man the gift of travel luggage for Valentine's Day, not his and hers, just his.
3. Every time he leaves stuff at your place, you stow it in a bag so you can get it back to him right away.
4. When he tells you his best friend is getting married, you smirk and respond, "Suckah!"
5. After he announces he's going away for a few days on business, you suggest he make it longer.

REMINDER CHECKLIST

1. Tune in to your inner voice: Is commitment in the cards for you?
2. Assess whether your guy is on board with your schedule. Make sure you and your boyfriend share the same fondness for your independence.
3. Write it down: What would a healthy relationship look like for you?
4. Share your blueprint with your man. Once you know what works for you, sit down and negotiate a plan as a couple.

(continued)

5. It's time to change your Outlook (calendar). Schedule set times to be together with your guy that you can both bank on.

6. Don't let others dictate your schedule. Remind yourself that you know what's right for you, so nobody else's two cents matters.

7. Schedule the Mom talk. Explain to your mother that you would like her to ask you about stuff in your life other than your relationship.

PART THREE

Changing Love-Life Goals

♥

This map is all confusing! I used
to be certain of my destination,
but now, after a few twists and turns,
I seem to be on a whole new path.

7

The Wedding Wisher

Definition: You suddenly find yourself fantasizing about marriage after a lifetime of not caring about it.

Pop Quiz

The song title that you most relate to is:

A Nancy Sinatra's "These Boots Are Made for Walking"
B Annie Lennox's "Sisters Are Doing It for Themselves"
C Bruce Springsteen's "I Wanna Marry You"

If you answered C, this chapter is for you.

RUTHIE'S STORY

"I was the woman who thought I was never going to get married," admits Ruthie,* 38. Instead, I was going to travel the world, freelance for magazines, meet exotic men, and have mind-blowing flings with them. People assume I feel this way because I had a rotten childhood and my parents had a terrible divorce, but it's not the case. My folks have a great marriage, going on forty years. I always just kind of walked to the beat of my own drum."

But this year Ruthie realized that she changed her mind; she wants to have a partner to go through life with. "I think part of it is that I'm watching my parents get older," she said, "and I'm going to have to make a lot of decisions about their health care soon. I can't count on my brother to help, and I don't want to do this alone. I want someone to lean on. Of course, I also want to be a support to my partner."

Ruthie has been dating a man for several months but isn't sure whether he's interested in marriage. "I don't want to spend the next few years of my life wondering if he'll propose to me," Ruthie said. She also admits she has started to nag him, demanding to know his intentions and blowing up at him when he says he isn't sure. "I sometimes feel like a shrew," Ruthie said, "but I don't want to waste time if he is not the right person."

Stage of Singlehood

Not until recently had you even considered the idea of marriage. Either you flat out never wanted to get hitched or you just didn't think about it. But you have changed your mind. Maybe you want to experience how your married friends are living; or you have decided you're now mature enough to commit to one person; perhaps you're feeling life truly would be better now with someone at your side. Whatever the reason, you're ready for this next step. The problem is, you have no prospects in mind for a husband and time is racing by, or you are with someone who is not interested in getting married right now and he thought you felt the same.

So how are you going to get him to change his mind? *Can* you get him to change his mind? The hard part is that the ball is going to be in his court, and you are going to feel relegated to the sidelines.

The Great News

You know what you want. It might not be what you thought, but that's fine. Our desires change all the time based on our personal experiences. What's important is being clear about your changing needs so you can make them happen. Hey, there are a lot of people ambling through life clued out to their own wants and can't figure out why they're miserable. Having redefined what you want for yourself, you're in a much better position to get it. In this case, you've decided you want to get married. I can't tell you when you'll meet your husband if you're dating; nor can I tell you whether the guy you're with currently is your Mr. Right (or whether it will be a lucky new fellow), but that's something you'll get closer to figuring out by using this chapter.

This is also an excellent opportunity for you to explore what it is about getting married that's so appealing to you right now. Maybe you're not exactly sure what changed; or you've decided you want to start a family; or you've been experiencing ramped-up pressure from people; or you've cultivated new fears about growing older alone. This chapter will also help you sort this out before you swap rings and life vows with another person. Understanding what's driving your new urge will help you make choices for yourself based on what is right for you rather than on fears and insecurities.

SHIFT YOUR THINKING

What's behind the quest for the ring?

Some of the women I interviewed told me that if they knew they were going to get married at *some* point, they wouldn't care so much that they weren't married now. If a fortune-teller said getting married was definitely in the cards, they would feel little pressure about it. As Hannah, 25, put it, "It's not that I want to get married right now or even in the next two or three years, I just want to know that it is going to happen."

Many more women told me they were tired of being the only unmarried woman among their friends. Their social life consisted mainly of invites from married friends to come over for a family barbecue or go to the playground with their friends' kids. It's fun on occasion but not exactly the ideal entertainment for a single woman. In fact, spending heaps of time with married friends can wear you down and make you feel that you haven't succeeded as a grown-up. *Is this the life you should be living?*

Annie, 30, for example, said, "I looked around and all my single friends were suddenly married and I was the last one standing. I suddenly wondered what was wrong with my boyfriend, and why he hadn't proposed to me. It wasn't something I ever worried about until I noticed that everyone else had paired off and got married by thirty."

Cynthia, 42, "got tired of being the only unmarried one in her set of friends." She says there were all these expectations for her to be the one who went to their house for visits because it was "too hard" for her married friends with kids to find time to come to her neighborhood. "Is it really that hard to find a couple hours once a month?" she wondered. She found herself, on the one hand, feeling good about not settling for the wrong guy, but on the other hand, wanting to be part of the married world with the rest of her friends, never to be the outcast again.

Erica,* 28, said, "I was happy with the way things were going with my boyfriend and felt no urge to marry—until the summer of 2008 when my mailbox got flooded with wedding invites from friends. There was this peer pressure to not get left behind—to get the engagement ring on my finger." Eventually, she and her boyfriend broke up "because we just weren't well-suited for each other, really," and Erica says she's relieved she didn't try to force a proposal, which she was heading toward. "Sure, I would have been married," she says, "but married and miserable."

So the first thing to figure out is where this urge to marry comes from. Is it the pressure to prove, like Annie, you are normal like your friends? Is it the desire, like Hannah, to know that it's going to happen *someday* so you can stop feeling so much angst about it now? Or is it that you really are just ready to settle down with a partner and don't want to waste time with Mr. Wrong when Mr. Right could be around the corner? Perhaps it's a combination of reasons, and you're not sure which one takes highest priority right now. It's time to find out.

The first way of sorting through your feelings is to explore whether there's anxiety around your new desire to get married and, if so, where it's coming from. Is it from a genuine place of wanting something you can't have right now, or is there more to it?

ACTION STEPS

 ### Write it down: What makes you anxious about not getting married?

Spend twenty to thirty minutes writing in your journal all the reasons you can think of, without censoring or crossing out answers. Go in depth when you can. Then, look at your list and see if one thing in particular stands out. Is someone pressuring you, and how are they doing it (is it blatant or subtle; what are they trying to tell you?)? What would happen if you never got married? What does a husband represent to you (would it prove something if you had one)? Are you looking for a man because you want to have a child in the near future? If it's clear that you are simply ready to say, "I do," then it's time to figure out how to proceed. If you are already in a committed relationship, you'll need to determine whether you and your guy are on the same page, so skip ahead to "Make an Act of Declaration to Your Guy."

Don't mistake first dates for husband auditions.

Dating when you're not interested in marriage is a very different animal than dating with "the ring" in mind. Sure, you have expectations of how you want to be treated and what the relationship will look like, but there is not a whole lot of pressure. If it doesn't work out, you end it. You may be disappointed, but you're not kicking yourself for losing precious time. When your heart is set on marriage, you are constantly aware of whether the men you date are husband material and how much time and energy you've invested in the relationship. You may also be more adamant about having clarity on the relationship and knowing where you stand at all times.

Alana, 33, for example, said, "My thoughts now about putting myself out there are conflicted and curious. I feel very strongly that I don't want to squander the opportunities I have now to maybe get married and have a baby. I don't have a lot of time left, and I don't want to look back at forty-five and think, 'Ugh, I didn't do it.'"

The truth is, guys *can* feel that energy and it is often hard for them to handle. One thirtysomething man I interviewed told me he's frustrated about dating women who seem to be on a beeline for getting married. He feels more like a checklist for husband potential than a guy on a date. Another thirtysomething told me that it is really hard to keep dating a woman who uses the term "settling down" on a *first* date. You may feel a ticking clock, but this is supposed to be a time of getting to know each other—and talking about more casual topics like favorite movies, travel dreams, and hobbies. It is not the time to throw down your desire to get married this year.

Know when to cut your losses and when to stick it out.

You should never hide the fact that you want to marry, but the first couple of dates are supposed to be about figuring out whether you even like each other. On the third date, if you're feeling potential with this person, it's okay to ask him what type of relationship he is looking for. Listen to his answer. If he tells you he's interested in finding the right person and settling down, great. You can continue getting to know each other better and in a variety of situations (for example, you're sick, he's sick, you're mad, he's depressed, you're around either—or both—of your families). I personally think women should also have a few good fights under their belt before they even think about whether they want to stay with a guy. Does he fight fair? Does he hold a grudge? Does he remain respectful when he's ticked off?

If he tells you he's not the marrying kind, end the relationship now before things get more serious. He's doing you a huge favor giving it to you straight. You are not going to change him and there is no point in spinning your wheels trying. Cut your losses and move on. If he tells you that he'd like to get married someday but he's not sure when, you can let him know that you are ready to marry as soon as you believe you have found the right person. If he looks panicky or can't look you in the eye, this is a bad sign and you may want to say, "It looks like we may be in two different places right now" and cut bait. If he stays neutral—nodding or saying, "Okay"—then it's up to you how much more time you want to invest in the relationship. It's certainly not fair to expect him to say he wants to marry you on date No. 4, but it's definitely reasonable as you approach the one-year mark.

Make an act of declaration to your guy.

If you're currently in a serious relationship, it may be time to state your needs more directly. I think many women believe their guy will intuit their sudden desire to marry and propose. Maybe you have started dropping what you consider to be not-so-subtle clues

("Oh, guess who's getting married?" "Do you like deejays or bands better?" "Who do you think will be your best man?"). You're letting him know you've got wedding on the brain, and it's impossible to miss. Yet the reality is, your guy may not have a clue because it's not on *his* brain. He's operating under the assumption that you aren't even thinking about marriage. So what's obvious to you isn't even near his radar.

That means if you don't come out with it, you are going to be waiting for a long time for a proposal, and storing up hurt and resentment. Instead of letting that happen, tell him directly that you want to marry and create a life with him. But that's so not romantic, some women will say, he needs to ask *me*. Yes, we'd rather have our men declare their love by spelling out "I love you" in rose petals and hiring skywriters to spell it out for all to see. But getting what you want is what's important and sometimes that means taking matters into your own hands. This is not to say that there aren't romantic and highly imaginative men out there who spend months conjuring up the perfect wedding proposal, or that you can't teach a man to act in romantic ways if he's open to it. You can't, however, expect your man to transform into one of these guys on his own if he's never been that way before.

In a blog posting called "Why Won't My Boyfriend Propose?" on The Female View (www.thefemaleview.com), an anonymous contributor suggests that rather than obsessing about a wedding proposal, "discuss finances, kids, dogs, and the house. It's always a good idea to make sure that you are both on the same mind-set and life path." If marriage is what you want, here's what she suggests: "Make the proposal easy for him by telling him that simple and sweet is better than paying out the wazoo to have the proposal written in the sky or posted on a billboard. By telling him what kind of proposal you want (in a nice, subtle way), it will ease his nerves about preparing the proposal."

This is a good place to mention that it is *not* the time for making ultimatums or idle threats. It may be tempting to tell your boyfriend, "Look, this is what I want, so you need to decide right now: Do you want to get married or break up?" The theory is, if he won't make a choice, you'll force him into it. Here's the problem: It's hard to make choices under duress. So even if he says, "Okay, let's get married," you are going to know for the rest of your life that it may have come from fear of losing you at that moment. Is that really how you want to enter a lifelong union with someone, with your guy proposing because he's scared? If he tells you he is going to choose "breakup" because he's not ready to marry, on the other hand, you may always wonder if it would have gone down like that had you approached it differently. Understand too that many people respond to a threat by bailing because they don't like being manipulated. No one wants to be bullied into offering up their heart.

Hear your guy's response, and not what you *want* to hear.

Once you are clear about what you want, ask your boyfriend what *he* wants for the future with you. What does he picture, and does he have a timeline? Next comes the hard part: listen to what he has to say (watch his body language too) without chiming in or twisting his words in your mind. Hopefully, he'll tell you exactly what you want to hear—that his plans include marrying you and sooner rather than later. If he tells you he hasn't given it much thought, hear that. If he says he's not marriage material, hear that too. Don't tell him why he's wrong or how you know he will change or how sorry he's going to be if he loses you. Just listen.

Also, if you're not clear on what he has said to you (most likely because he's fumbling through this or stalling for time or caught off guard), ask him gently if he could better explain his thoughts (not "Can you clarify what the hell you're talking about?!" but rather "I want to be clear on what you're telling me. Are you saying that . . .?"). You are gathering information, not making a decision right now. Take deep breaths and remind yourself of this, as many times as you need to.

One 38-year-old single had this to say: "My boyfriend is not sure he wants to get married and have children. He wants a career and a house but he says children are too big of a responsibility. I'm teed off. We've been together for three years. I am getting old and won't have time for children. I mean, how long should I sit around waiting for him to decide?"

If you are in this situation as well, know that your boyfriend *has* decided. He doesn't want to marry you right now. If he wants to get hitched it's not going to be anytime soon. Clearly he knows you want to marry (because you told him); the fact that he isn't proposing means that he is not on the same page. You can mold the story however you like ("Well, he'll change his mind when all his friends get married," or "If I go out of town for a little while he'll see he can't be without me"), but it is far saner to deal with reality. That way you can hurt now and move on rather than hashing out this same conversation in upcoming months or even years and resenting how much more time you have wasted. Staying with him at this point may be a bit like expecting a cow to produce juice—a novel idea that's just not going to happen.

Give yourself a time-out.

If you don't hear an affirming yes to marriage from your man, don't say or do anything rash. It's not in your best interest to scream obscenities or stomp out of the room. Instead, take a deep breath and tell him that you'd like to think over this conversation. If he wants to know what the problem is or why you're acting all weird, tell him straight out, "I was hoping we'd be in the same place, but we're clearly not, so I need some time to think about this and how I feel about it."

This is not meant to be a political strategy or threat. You *should* think about this conversation and how you want to handle it. Give yourself time to reflect on what he's said and how you feel about the news. What if he doesn't want to get married to you? What will that mean? What if he wants to commit to living together but not legally wedding? What if he would like more time to figure it out? What's acceptable to you? What feels *good* to you? What do you feel entitled to?

Spend this time deciding what you can/cannot live with. It may include a few variations. There may be a Plan A (he says he wants to get married and everything works out like you envisioned) and a Plan B (he says he's not ready to commit and you break up with him); or Plan C (he needs more time and you tell him that you will wait, but not forever). What's important is that you don't want to use this info as a maneuver to get your way. You want to get to a place that feels like you are honoring your integrity so you know that no matter what the outcome is, you walk away with your true self intact.

When I turned thirty, I told my boyfriend flat out that I wanted to get married in the next couple of years, and I was sure he would agree. It was kind of a given to me, and I was letting him know I would accept his proposal. So when he said he'd have to think about that, I was shocked. Think about *what*? What had we been doing—playing house together for two years?! But I just said okay and gave him some time to process instead. He ended up telling me he wasn't ready and we broke up. It was brutal, but I have no regrets in how I handled it. I allowed myself to see what had to be seen. Now I'm married to someone else who was excited to marry me and didn't need to be convinced.

Nancy,* 30, says one of the hardest and most valuable days of her life was when she asked her boyfriend whether he was ready to commit to her or not and, as she put it, "he got all flustered and red-faced and started rambling about how it was a bad time and maybe someday but not right now." Nancy said she knew deep down that the answer was no, and that she had to really listen to that, even when it was tempting to push it away and give him more time so he would change his mind. She sat with the news for a few days and gathered her strength and then told him, "I know that we love each other, but I also know that I'm going to grow to resent you very quickly if we stay together like this, so I am going to leave." That's exactly what she did. She packed up her stuff and moved out. "He kept telling me that I should stay and maybe he'd be ready soon and I was giving up and all this stuff. But I knew this time I had to go with my gut." According to Nancy, she has never looked back and it ended up being one of her proudest moments.

It doesn't always end in a breakup, by the way. Certainly friends of mine had happier endings with their men after heavy-duty emotional discussions. There were surprise proposals and even appreciation down the road from guys who said they just needed a little push to get them there. You can't know how your guy is going to respond or how it's going to turn out. But you can take satisfaction in knowing that you handled the situation well and got the information you needed to make the best choice you could at the time.

Tune in to your inner voice: Should you invest more time in your relationship?

Sit quietly and ask yourself, "Am I okay about not having plans to marry my boyfriend or am I resentful?" See what answer comes up for you without trying to change it. Once you know the answer, you will be much better prepared for a conversation with him.

Don't throw down a deadline, you don't need it.

It may be that your man tells you he is on the same page with you relationship-wise but is not ready to propose *right now*. Maybe he needs to get his business off the ground, or make a change in his life, or take care of something or someone first. Whatever it is, he asks you for more time and, let's say, that's okay with you for a little while. So how do you know when it's *too* much time? Should you give him a deadline now? Should you set a D-day on your calendar to end things with him?

While a deadline can feel safe, a definitive marker, I think it is often a mistake. For one thing he is going to feel "under the gun," and once again you're going to get an answer from him based on fear or anxiety, which is a rough way to start a marriage.

If you give yourself a deadline (one month, two months, whatever), it's an arbitrary number anyway. The point is how you feel now, not in the future. I'm much more in favor of women trusting themselves to know when enough is enough by checking in with themselves regularly; if and when there comes a time when your inner voice tells you that resentment outweighs being with him, you just hit your deadline.

It may be that you need to schedule check-ins with yourself every set amount of time (say, every three or four weeks) until knowing how you feel comes naturally to you. Your inner voice may tell you that things feel pretty good in terms of your relationship and you're not feeling any rush; it may say that it's feeling a little worse than it was; or it may tell you that you're becoming more and more resentful, which is causing the relationship to dive south. At that point, it's time to get out.

One friend of mine, who recently broke up, told me that she knew for about two months that her boyfriend was not going to commit to her. Every time she went to break up with him, however, he would plan something really romantic and make her feel so special that she would postpone the breakup. "I wanted to believe that his gestures were showing me that he was committed, but I knew in my heart of hearts that he just didn't want to break up. Two months later, I could no longer ignore my gut," she said, "which was screaming this guy was a commitment-phobe. The longer I stayed with him, the less time I would have to find the right person to build a life with." This friend did finally call things off with him and, while she misses the romance and intimacy, she knows she did the right thing for herself.

End the relationship when it's over.

If you, too, reach this point when you know it's time to walk, follow that reaction. In fact, if just reading this makes you feel a twinge of relief, there is a good chance you're there already. Tell your boyfriend that as much as you care for him, this relationship is no longer working for you. Be clear, be calm, and be firm—and only have this conversation when you're really ready to leave and not as a ploy.

Do not get stuck in the drama if he tells you that this is all your fault or that he has really been working on his issues or he's getting closer. He may or may not believe that when he says it; in either case, it doesn't matter. He is not where you need him to be. Wanting to stay with you is not the same as being ready to marry you.

Let him know that you are done waiting and wish him the best. There is no reason to rehash the conversation over and over, even if he's crying and telling you he can change or that you're acting hysterical. Gather your belongings and go, and then congratulate yourself for standing up for your own needs and being true to who you are. That doesn't mean that you are going to want to throw a victory party. More likely, you have a stretch of grieving ahead of you. But working through this sadness is a thousand times better than feeling like you've compromised who you are because you were afraid to be alone. You did the right thing, and chose to value yourself rather than getting driven by fear.

Surround yourself with extrastrength support.

If you do decide to stay with your boyfriend because that feels right, come up with surefire ways to handle friends and family telling you it's time to settle down. They may be asking you what you're waiting for and/or accusing you of not stepping up. They may blame your boyfriend and tell you that a real man would have asked you to get married by now. Maybe they just don't understand why you and your boyfriend aren't married, when most of the people they know are. Whether people are making subtle comments or creating a full-on offensive, it has to stop. It's hard enough to navigate your needs sometimes without having others feed your insecurities and attack your confidence. You can even go so far as to let these folks know that marriage is not on the table for discussion anymore. It's something you and your boyfriend are figuring out and you'll do it in private.

Another way to lessen your inner pressure to marry is to create a network of people who have your back; that way, you're not feeling so reliant on a husband to fill that role. If you worry about getting older and enduring more health issues either with yourself or with family members, for instance, you need to know there are others on standby to help. Like Ruthie in the opening story, you may find it tempting to stay with your man, even if he's not the right one, because you want to be with *someone* to help make the tough decisions ("Should I consider putting my mom in assisted living?" "Do I need to hire a nurse to help my father during the nights?"). That is why you need to set up a support group who will stand by your side when you're feeling vulnerable and scared.

What kind of support group might alleviate your fears? If you're anxious about getting sick or making important family decisions by yourself, ask your closest friends and/or relatives if they would be willing to help you. Discuss what you might need from them (a lift to the hospital, driving to the drugstore for medication, help with researching medical options, a listening ear) so you have the security of knowing there is a plan in place ("If I need to get to the hospital, Mary Ann will be the point person I can call who takes me there." "If I have to make decisions about my father's heart condition, I will call my best friend to help me research the options." "I will call my therapist to talk through how I feel about the options").

A 41-year-old nurse told me via e-mail that her worst moment of being single was "taking myself to the emergency room after ten p.m. on a weeknight. I had to have some sedation to have an abscess drained. The doctor asked me how I got there, and I told him I drove myself. He asked if I could get anyone to pick me up because of the narcotic medicine he needed to give me for the procedure, and I briefly thought about it and said no. Maybe there were people I could have called in a dire emergency, but lots of my friends go to bed early and I didn't feel comfortable waking them. So I had to wait until the sedative wore off, then drove myself at one a.m. to find a twenty-four hour pharmacy to fill my own prescription, only to have to go pick it up at six a.m. before going to work the next day. I felt really alone."

This should never, ever happen to anyone. If I found out one of my single friends drove herself to or from the hospital instead of calling me, I would be horrified. In fact, I'd like to think this nurse's friends told her that it was ludicrous she didn't call them. Have at least one or two friends be your backup. Knowing you don't have to go it alone may alleviate some of your stress— and remind you that there is emotional and practical support a phone call away. They may ask for you to provide the same support for them, which will even further tighten the bond.

Write it down: How can you eliminate
fears of being alone during
an emergency?

Spend twenty minutes or so jotting down ideas in your journal
for steps you can take to feel more in control. These may include
signing up for a prescription medical service so pills can be delivered to your house if you need, having the phone numbers of
physicians handy, writing down the address of the nearest emergency room and number for a taxicab just in case, listing the
phone numbers of your support-network friends (their cell and
home numbers).

Hopefully, having this plan in place will help you feel stronger
and more confident about being able to take care of yourself. You
know you'll be fine whether you marry or not. If you're going to
stand under the altar and exchange vows with a partner, it should
come from wanting to spend your life with him, and not from a
place of wanting to secure future help.

Schedule the Mom talk: Request more emotional support, less wedding talk.

It's so easy for your mother to get swept away knowing that you
are hoping for a big formal wedding. Of course, it's tempting to
tell her that you are starting to get itchy for marriage and have
been considering what guests you would invite. You know she'll
get caught up in the joyful frenzy of planning and you want to
share this moment with her, have a mother-daughter bonding
ritual. The problem is, once you open that box of possibility with

your mom, it's doubtful you can close it. For a lot of mothers, once you say "wedding day" she's on the phone the next day with florists, caterers, and every local band in your town or city.

You are dealing with enough frustration right now in figuring out whether your boyfriend is going to take the plunge. The last thing you need is your mother bringing up the future wedding every other phone call with more and more questions and tips. Don't bring up a potential wedding until your man pops the question and you say yes.

If your mom keeps nagging you about when that boyfriend of yours is going to propose and/or asks what is taking so long, set boundaries. Tell her, "I know you want me to be happy and to watch me get married, but right now we are not there. I will let you know when that changes, but until then, I would really appreciate it if you would drop the wedding talk."

 ## In case of emergency: Get out of the house!

If you find yourself wanting to throw down a threat to your guy to propose, exit the building. It's normal to have moments of infuriation because you're not getting what you want, and there's nothing you can do to change it. You can't make your man be where you need him to be, and perhaps you feel the pressure of a ticking clock exacerbating the situation. During these very human moments, the best thing you can do is take a breather by going for a walk, working out, meditating, whatever helps you calm down. Ultimatums provide great drama in TV shows and movies, but never work in real life. Meet up with your boyfriend again only once you've ditched the urge to "deadline" him.

$ TEAR UP THE CARDS

Some women find themselves desperate to marry because they are financially strapped. Maybe you have credit card debt and the idea of marrying someone means you're not going to end up on the streets collecting cans for cash. The best thing you can do is take care of your own credit card debt now, because it's not your guy's responsibility whether you end up marrying or not. Take a deep breath and tear up your credit cards. They're history, so let them go. Then, as financial experts suggest, find a way to pay back the credit card with the highest interest first and work your way down. If you don't know where to start, call the Consumer Credit Counseling Service at 1-800-388-2227, where you can get help organizing and consolidating your debt.

6 CLUES YOU'RE OBSESSED WITH MARRIAGE

1. You start spending Saturday afternoons trying on wedding gowns and when the owner asks when the big day is, you sing out, "Sooooooooon."
2. Rather than finishing your office report, you're chatting with brides on wedding forums about floral arrangements.
3. You spend countless hours perusing wedding registries, obsessing about whether you want a white floral vase or the peach one.

(continued)

4. You host a dinner party for your girlfriends, and serve wedding cake for dessert.

5. At your hair salon, you now look around for what hairstyles you want everyone in your bridal party to don on the big day.

6. Your friends start telling you they'd love to hang but they have to "get that thing checked" on their car.

 ## REMINDER CHECKLIST

1. Write it down: What makes you anxious about not getting married?

2. Don't mistake first dates for husband auditions. Don't let your desire to get married sabotage your dates.

3. Know when to cut your losses and when to stick it out. Make sure your relationship is working for you now, not possibly in the future.

4. Make an act of declaration to your guy. If you're committed to a man, be clear with him on your desire to marry.

5. Hear your guy's response, and not what you *want* to hear. Pay attention to your guy's answers or you'll end up spinning your wheels.

6. Give yourself a time-out. Take whatever time you need to process his response instead of blurting out your gut reaction.

7. Tune in to your inner voice: Should you invest more time in your relationship?

8. Don't throw down a deadline, you don't need it.

9. End the relationship when it's over. Pack your bags (or his) when you realize the idea of breaking up would be kind of a relief.

10. Surround yourself with extrastrength support. Create a network of people who have got your back.

11. Write it down: How can you eliminate fears of being alone during an emergency?

12. Schedule the Mom talk: Tell your mother you could use her emotional support—but not her wedding suggestions right now.

13. In case of emergency: Get out of the house!

8

The Town Rebel

Definition: You no longer aspire to live the cookie-cutter lifestyle (husband, two kids, one dog), which means that you stick out like a sore thumb in your community.

Pop Quiz

When people in your hometown hear you're still single, they:

A Look at you like your house just burned to the ground.
B Switch topics and ask about your job.
C Give you a bone-crushing hug and yell, "Good for you, honey!"

If you answered A, this chapter is for you.

JILLIAN'S STORY

Jillian,* 26, grew up assuming that she would get married because "it was just the thing you do." All the people she knew in her

Southern community were married by age twenty-four and she never considered any other options. It was only when she went off to college that she first started meeting women her own age who didn't assume marriage was the next step.

"I was completely fascinated by this group of women I was hanging out with," Jillian recalls. "They wanted to be artists like me and they seemed comfortable with the idea of being on their own. It was during this time that Jillian realized that she didn't want to marry any time soon, either. Instead, she wanted to focus on her painting and maybe get married down the road. The problem, she said, was that when she returned to her hometown after college, she felt trapped. "I moved back home to be close to my nieces and nephews, whom I adore," said Jillian. "But the cost of being here is that it's going to get harder and harder to find eligible men if I keep waiting. Plus, I'm going to be the town freak show."

Stage of Singlehood

You are living in a place where the town motto might as well be "Settled down by thirty," and it's starting to do you in. Maybe you're here because it's always been home, and like it or not, this is where your family is rooted. Or maybe you're here for a specific opportunity that you couldn't forgo. In either case, you feel like the town weirdo, "the outsider." It's bad enough knowing you stick out from everyone else, as the old spinster, but people in the community are not shy about letting you know that your relationship status is unacceptable. Instead of celebrating, or at least tolerating, that you are choosing the less traveled path, they just want to fix you. As time goes on, you're starting to feel more and more stuck. You want out, but what's the cost of bailing?

The Great News

You are not stuck. It is easy to feel that way when the only reason you are living where you do is because you have a specific obligation or there's a unique situation that calls for it. You never would have picked this place off the map to be your home, but here you are. When you put everything on the scale and weigh what is important, life may tip toward living in this locale for now—but that is still a choice and not the same as being stuck. Know that if the scale tips too far in the other direction—and life as a single woman becomes treacherous—you can leave. Really. It may not be a fly-by-night experience where you pack up your suitcase and hit the open roads at midnight, but you will concoct a thoughtful exit out.

In the meantime, there are definitely strategies for making life easier while you are here (that don't include mail-order husband shopping). There are ways to take part in community events without fearing you'll be ridiculed or judged. Heck, you may even want to think of this time as an opportunity to expose the locals to your "alternative" lifestyle and help them see that, yes, singles are people too. It's not your job to be the town educator, but why not take advantage of the opportunity and make it easier for the next generation of girls who won't want to marry early? Thanks to modern technology, there is also a whole support system out there—just one click away to people who feel just like you (more on this later).

SHIFT YOUR THINKING

Are you where you need to be?

There's no doubt that most of the single women over the age of twenty-five whom I interviewed were living in big cities among thousands, if not millions, of other single women. They had their share of disappointments and frustrations over being single in the city, but they never had to deal with being the town spinster. All they have to do if they are feeling lonely or isolated is saunter downtown to remember that they are in extremely good company. Those who were raised in small towns or communities with traditional values typically took the first bus out of Dodge the moment they saved up enough cash.

Take Leslie, 34. She told me that she used to define "happily ever after" as "barefoot, pregnant, cooking meals—you know, the traditional Beaver Cleaver family." People settled down early in her suburban Massachusetts town, so that's what she knew. But since taking a job in downtown Boston, she now dreams of "a nice living and an international vacation a year." Unfortunately, she says, she still "gets pressure from everyone back home," including "a grandma who has been at me since I was eighteen to find the right man."

Lauren, 25, a single from Minnesota who performs with her band around the country, said, "I definitely feel pressure to get married when I'm back home, and not a little. All my friends are married, and so you start to question when it's going to happen for you, if it's going to happen. It's different being single in the Midwest than in a big city because it's much slower paced and almost everyone marries early—most of my friends married in their early twenties."

What's different for you is that you're residing, at least temporarily, in a community where it's considered just plain sad if you're single. You know your reason for sticking it out. Maybe you are staying home to help out a family member until he or she can get back on his or her feet. Maybe you've hit a rough patch of economic luck and are living back home until you can regroup. Perhaps the best school or job training for what you want to do is located in this part of the country. Whatever your reason, the first question to ask yourself, assuming you're unhappy in this location, is what exactly is keeping you here? Is the reason compelling enough for you to stay? If yes, then you will clearly need to figure out ways to fit in while you are here and ways to build relationships.

Maybe you are living in this place because you grew up here and can't imagine starting over somewhere new where you don't know a soul; or you don't feel like you have the energy to pack your bags and go set up a whole new life somewhere else. One thing is certain: it's not by accident you are living here. So it's time to ask yourself why you're putting down roots in town, and if it's in your best interest at this moment to stay. If it *is*, at least temporarily, then it's essential to find ways to nourish your sense of well-being and not get caught in waiting for happiness *someday*.

ACTION ITEMS

 Tune in to your inner voice: Does it make sense for you to stay put?

Find a quiet spot, close your eyes, and ask yourself whether it makes more sense for you to be living where you do now or to pack up and go. Don't worry about what you should do or what's reasonable; just listen to what responses pop up.

If your inner voice reports back that remaining in this community and completing your journey here is the best idea, then it's important that you know that. It is your *choice*, and hopefully the suggestions in this chapter will make your time here more enjoyable.

For those of you living in the "wrong" place for now in order to accomplish a specific task or goal (say, helping your mother through an illness, finishing grad school, or getting some type of unique training), remind yourself regularly that this is temporary. Also, know deep down that if living here becomes too unbearable, there are ways out. Some of you may realize that it no longer makes sense for you to be here. Spending the next several years in misery for the potential benefit of the future may be too much to ask. There are no black-and-white answers on how much time is too much, but many women live in extremely compromised situations because they do not want to be regarded as quitters or failures. Looking out for your well-being is not the sign of a quitter; it is the sign of a woman with good instincts. How do you know quitting is the right decision? I like how simply Alisa Bowman put it in her blog, Project Happily

Ever After: "When you do quit, you'll experience one sensation: relief."

You may find that your thoughts about living in this community are changing all the time; in fact, riding the ups and downs of being here is what's perpetually zapping your energy. One day, it seems quaint and charming in town and you appreciate the easygoing pace, the next day it seems overbearing.

Melissa, 29, lives in Sarasota, Florida, and says she loves the sunshine, the art, being on the water, and hanging out with her girlfriends. But dating is extremely challenging for her. "When I first moved here," she said, "I met some friends who warned me that all the guys here are over fifty and I didn't really believe them. I figured there are young single guys everywhere and it will not be a problem. But they were right, most guys are older here. The ones that are younger are recent transplants from other parts of the country who moved here to escape something back home. So they come here to start a new life and, frankly, they don't have their s*** together." How Melissa feels about Sarasota depends on the day and whether she just experienced a brutal date that confirmed her worries about the men there.

One fortysomething college professor said she moved to a small midwestern town because of the cheaper cost of living and getting paid $30,000 more than she was currently being paid. But there was an emotional cost to that move. As she put it, "I've met a substantial number of women who think I'm just waiting for them to turn their backs so I can pounce on their men, drag them back to my house, and do depraved, undoubtedly perverted, and possibly illegal things to their bodies. This makes me grin. Some of the men think I'm waiting for an opportunity too. This makes me roll my eyes. Admittedly, it's a novelty for me to be seen as some sort of wanton hussy, but the charm of it has grown pale. I'm tired of women grabbing their husbands' arms when I walk by, and I'm very tired of having to stop myself from snarking, 'Oh, *really* . . . who the hell wants your husband anyway, aside from you?'"

When all your time is being spent navigating the ups and downs of living in a particular place, it's easy to forget to consider whether you *should* stay where you are. On the one hand, no place is perfect; on the other hand, there has to be a better place for you than this small town. Keep assessing your feelings over time and not just on particularly stressful or wonderful days. If you look back after a few months and see that the draining days of living in a marriage-obsessed community far outnumber the good days, it may be a tip-off that it's time to pack your Samsonite luggage.

 ## Write it down: What are the pros and cons of living in your community?

Still not quite sure whether you should remain here? Write a list in your journal of every good and bad thing about living where you do. When you're done, see whether there are more pros or cons on the list. Mind you, not every item counts the same: if you're living at home because your dad is recovering from surgery and needs help, that is obviously more important than "I miss Ethiopian food." But it's important to distinguish exactly how much you are compromising by living here. Also, in having this list, you can start to distinguish what you can and can't control, so you can begin planning ways to alleviate, or at least minimize, the problems that you can control (you'll find plenty of ideas below). Seeing the list on paper—rather than just thinking it in your head—can be helpful in organizing and prioritizing your concerns.

Make your escape plan . . . just in case.

As mentioned above, maybe you grew up in this town, went to school here, and found a job. You're here because you could never imagine going anywhere else, this is home. Sure, it's hard to deal with the fact that most of your friends have married, but the idea of ditching home is daunting. Perhaps you're here for one of the other reasons listed above. No matter what it is, one thing's for sure, there are days when you fantasize about calling Greyhound for a one-way ticket out.

Daisy, 35, lives in New Haven, Connecticut, and loves her job working at an organization that aims to "improve the urban appeal" of her town. She writes an entertaining newsletter for them and says she loves doing this work. But she's lived in this relatively small city for years and fears "there are no guys left to meet." She feels like she knows just about all of the single men in her age group, and many guys in town are "age inappropriate because they're here for college [Yale]." She worries she's "never going to meet anyone new here, even just to date" and sometimes thinks she should head to a bigger city.

If you, too, sometimes dream of the big escape, come up with a plan. Should you decide to ditch this place, what would you need to do? Would you have to save up money for a while? Do extensive relocation research? Find job openings to apply to? Visit other cities to see where you might fit in? First things first: let yourself dream of where you want to be. It doesn't mean you have to do anything right now, but putting a plan in place will make it that much easier to leave if and when you do decide you've had enough.

 ## Write it down: Where can you imagine relocating?

Spend ten minutes recording in your journal some parts of the country you're interested in exploring. Practice saying aloud, "Oh, I'm moving to Chicago," or "Yes, I live in Portland." How does it feel? If you get overwhelmed by choices, explore a map and see what areas of the country may call to you. Jot down the location and what intrigues you most about the area. You're not committing to anywhere—you're just opening possibilities. Then start writing answers to the following questions:

- What finances would you need to make the move?
- What is the cost of living in the areas you're interested in?
- Where would you most likely be able to find work?
- Do you know anyone in the area you're exploring who could answer questions?
- How many singles live in the population of that place?

You don't have to figure all this out in one sitting; it may be something you work on whenever you're feeling frustrated and stuck. You keep fleshing out a plan, making it more and more conceivable and less of a pipe dream. The point of this exercise is to help you appreciate that there are real alternatives for you if and when you're ready to go. The more research you put into moving now, the easier it will be when you decide the time is right.

Make like a horror movie character and "get out of the house."

For now, regardless of your list, you are living here—and it may be tempting to hibernate in order to avoid the endless judgment, irritating questions, and nosy neighbors. Plus your place brings the temptations of your comfy couch, the latest episodes of *The Real Housewives of New York City*, and all the creature comforts you need. Why leave? Here's why: because holing up in your house is not a long-term option to a sane life. Whether you're going to be living in this location for one more month or for who knows how long, you need to form friendships. (The characters you've been following on your favorite TV show are *not* your real friends.)

Maybe you're thinking, "Yeah, but there's no one for me to connect with out there. It's all married couples with kids, who want me to be married too. What's the point?" The point is, whether the adults are married or not, there are things you can talk about with these people—and it's flat-out unhealthy to stay isolated. Says Hara Estroff Marano in a *Psychology Today* article called "The Dangers of Loneliness," "Friendship is a lot like food. We need it to survive. What is more, we seem to have a basic drive for it. Psychologists find that human beings have fundamental need for inclusion in group life and for close relationships. We are truly social animals. The upshot is, we function best when this social need is met. It is easier to stay motivated, to meet the varied challenges of life."

You already have plenty of challenges on your plate, namely trying to fit into a community that doesn't know what to make of a single person your age. You need companionship, and it's time to make finding it a priority in your life. You'll be surprised at how fantastic it feels to connect with people again.

For Jamie,* 34, life turned around when she befriended a married woman her age with two kids. "I never thought that we would have anything to talk about because we were at such different stages of life," she said. "But we went out for drinks one night and she told me that she was actually really jealous of my life and missed the freedom to do whatever she wanted. It was such a gift she gave me, reminding me of the value of being single when everywhere I looked people were married. I guess she reminded me that marriage doesn't equal happiness. And I was able to open up to her about how hard it was to be single in this town. We confessed some deep stuff that night, and we've been close friends ever since."

Another single woman, who moved to a small town in Texas, told me that life got better when she joined a book club that included several divorced women in town. "I didn't think I'd have much in common with divorcées, but they knew how hard it was to live in our town with no one to bring to the family picnics or holiday parades or other outings. Plus, they had to deal with seeing their exes around town. Honestly, it made being single seem less stressful. It was also just nice to open up and connect with these women."

Widen your search past town boundaries.

Unquestionably, there are challenges that come from dating in small towns: everyone knows your business, the pool of eligible guys is small, and if you make one horrible misstep during your date (like spraying soda out your nose when you laugh), chances are high that the rest of the town is going to know about it by Tuesday.

Debbie,* age 38, from a small town of about 30,000, said, "If you can't find guys at work or in church, then good luck finding a guy."

Yes, it's true, you don't have the scores of meeting spots you have in a big city. But the truth is, sometimes it can be easier to make connections in Small Town, U.S.A. People in cities don't always give each other the benefit of the doubt or get to really know each other because there are millions of other singles right there to choose from; people sometimes seem more disposable. Also, in cities you're not likely to run into the really attractive guy you saw yesterday at the deli *again*, but in a small town it's a given.

Remind yourself that you are not limited by the men in your particular town. Expand your search to neighboring areas and anyplace that's within an hour-long drive (or longer if you can hack it). How do you find guys in these other places? Use online dating websites where you can tick off how many miles you are willing to travel for a date; ask people in your town for suggestions, or make a point of signing up for a hiking club or other activity in a nearby location.

As a bonus, remember that if you are a city girl who's moved to this town, you carry a certain cache or mystique. I love what this anonymous woman posted on a dating forum called "Big City vs. Small Town" on www.city-data.com: "Guys were chomping at the bit to go out with the rarity . . . a young, educated, degreed professional female who didn't come with a passel of kids already, living in a small, rural town. I had scarcity value, it was a rare thing. In an urban area, that's not so rare." Take pride in your novelty, and let your exotic glamour wash over the eligible men in town.

Go scouting for townfolk.

So how can you find guys right in your own neck of the woods? Unless you live so far in the sticks that there are literally no places of business (and what are you *doing* there?), you'll likely be able to track down men at the locations below. Also, be on the lookout for one or two potential friends—or at least acquaintances who you can go to the movies with or meet for coffee to chat about your day.

 A fitness center: Everyone needs to get in shape, right? The benefit, of course, is that even if no one will talk to you while you're there, you at the very least are going to get physically fit. (That's a hundred times better than sitting in a dingy bar staring at the door to see who might possibly walk in that doesn't look like a delinquent.) The other thing about fitness centers is that they often plan group events, such as neighborhood runs, volleyball games, and tennis tournaments. The fact that you're a new member gives you an instant excuse to talk to anybody you want ("Excuse me, do you know where the racquetball courts are? I've never been here before," "Can you tell me if there is any place to buy snacks here?" "Could you help me up? I just fell off the treadmill.").

 The local supermarket: I don't care how small your town is, there is a grocery store or some kind of market. If there are single folk, you're going to see them shopping most likely on weekends. Use the opportunity to go up to people your age and ask them questions, letting them know you're new to the community. You don't want to be a creepy girl desperate for a new friend, just a nice new gal in town who hasn't had a chance to meet anyone yet. Put a smile on your face and ask someone (not a man wearing a gold band, preferably) a question. It can be anything from "Excuse me, do you know how late this place is open?" to "I've just moved here, and I'm wondering what people do for entertainment in this town." One or two people may blow you off, but most will understand the vulnerable position you just put yourself and show some kindness.

Town events: Most small towns hold annual events that bring people in the community together several times a year. It might be a race, a town fair, a blood donor drive, a sports event, community theater, or something else. If in your head you are already making snarky comments right now, get over yourself. You are the one who needs company so get out there and try. If all the people over eighteen are married, befriend them anyway and let them know you're single and looking.

A few other suggestions for small-town meeting places: the local coffee shop (there are caffeine addicts everywhere), church or synagogue, adult education classes, lectures, and bookshops. And, of course, there's the local quilting bee (just kidding).

Get off the defensive.

As you start meeting more and more people in your community, you will prove to them that you're not going to steal the local men or kidnap the womenfolk's babies. Seriously, you may be the first person over a certain age in your community who's not married, so your neighbors don't know what to expect or how to talk to you.

They may have questions: "How come you never got married?" "Don't you ever get lonely?" "Do you feel sad about being single?" It would be easy to mistake these comments as judgmental, patronizing, and even downright bitchy. It is more likely these questions will come from people trying to understand you better. In their eyes, you get married and have babies while you're young. That's just what you do. You're throwing off the system and they are trying to understand why. That doesn't mean that you have to give them an essay-length explanation of why you are single, but you can let them know: "I haven't found anyone who feels like the right fit" or "I'm not willing to settle down with the wrong person."

Surely they are going to have plenty of questions or comments in response, and it's your decision how many of them you are willing to answer. If you start feeling uncomfortable or defensive, change the subject ("We'll see. Now tell me about your photography, how long have you been doing it?" or "It'll all work out. Hey, when's the town picnic this summer?"). If that doesn't work, just tell them they'll be among the first to know if and when you meet your match.

Shake up your perspective.

It's easy to have dark days when you're reminded over and over that others believe there is something dreadfully wrong with you. There would have to be if no one is willing to marry you (that's the implicit belief, isn't it?). Even if you know you're fine, it can be hard to remember on days when you feel like the lone solo on Noah's ark. This is a perfect time to remind yourself that the grass isn't always greener on the other side.

One twenty-seven-year-old from North Carolina told me it was helpful "listening to a friend complain about her marriage and realizing that friend isn't happy. I was unhappy for my friend and wanted her to be happy, but I was glad not to be in her shoes."

In an online article called "When Everyone Else is Married," Stacey Goldstein admitted, "I spent hours alone on my couch, wondering what was wrong with me. Everyone else was married, had a house, a job, and was about to have a child. I had none of these things. What was my problem? Why didn't I have anything at all? These were difficult days. Days spent alone with my thoughts, comparing myself to my friends' lives and coming up short. Days wondering why I was such a societal freak."

What changed things for her, she said, was getting out of her own head and really looking at the lives of her friends who were cranking out babies. "My highly intelligent, fun, competent friends were reduced to zombielike, unshowered, sleepwalking, milk dispensers. Their every thought and every move centered around their babies. They could barely function. The more I saw of this kind of life, the less interested I was in having it as my own. From my point of view, it looked pretty terrible."

Soon Stacey found a complete appreciation for her life: "I want to keep having my own fun. I want nights filled with deep sleep, not screaming. I want to go to dinner at seven p.m. like a normal person. I don't want to spend all my money on day care. Seeing how other people's lives completely change when they get married and have children makes me cling to my own life. I appreciate it the way it is—filled with mundane experiences that belong to me."

When you are having one of those days where perspective takes a hiatus, make sure you don't take it out on the locals. Says Laura Schaefer in her article "How to Find Love in a Small Town," "Any town, big or small, has its share of frustrations for its residents. But whether you're on a date or just chatting with someone at the hardware store, try to keep your more negative views to yourself, whether that's 'This place is so boring,' 'I don't know why I live here,' or 'I'm going to move as soon as _____.'" To you, it might seem like you're making casual conversation. To locals, you've just insulted how they choose to live their lives. Find somewhere else to bring the critique. Write it in your journal, call a close friend who is living somewhere else, express yourself through art, or punch a pillow, but don't be a town "hater" to the townspeople.

Schedule the Mom talk: Let her know how tiring it is being the outcast.

If you grew up in a small community, then there is a decent chance that your mother sees the wedding and babies as a given by age twenty-five. Thirtysomething Dahlia said about her mom, "She is from Israel and she married early, and she thinks that marrying is the only thing that will make me happy. She can't think beyond that framework!" For mothers like this, it's not only sad you are single, it is a worrisome reflection on how she mothered you. If just about every other woman your age is strolling the streets with a husband and a stroller, why not you? Where did it all go wrong?

The first thing you can do is assure your mother that you being single has nothing to do with how she raised you. You can even let her know, if it's true, that you thought you'd be married by now as well. But for whatever reason you feel differently now and you no longer want a life that feels essentially cookie-cutter. You can also let her know that in spite of her disappointment you would really appreciate her support, given how hard it is to deal with judgment from everyone else.

Tell her, "I want to continue to build our relationship with you as adults, but that can only happen if I feel that you respect my decision to stay single right now. You don't have to agree with it, you just have to respect that I can make my own decisions. And I will respect the fact that marriage is important to you and not say anything about it that you might find offensive or hurtful."

Then make sure that you don't use your mom as an emotional dumping ground when you're feeling bad about being single. You already know she's worried about you, so don't give her more reasons to be upset about your relationship status. Instead, talk to friends who can empathize with what you're going through and give you an emotional boost.

Log on to the Internet and connect with singles.

It used to be that if you were single in a community where everyone paired off early, you were socially screwed. With the Internet, you've got an entire community of like-minded people at the touch of your fingertips. This means, thanks to online dating sites, the chance to meet men from a town or two over who you might never have met. But there is another gift you can take advantage of, and that's forums for singles. An Internet connection means getting to talk to thousands of single women who are experiencing the same hopes and disappointments that you are going through, for free and without having to jump on a plane. Take advantage of this amazing opportunity. Just by researching this book and putting in requests to interview people on forums, I've heard from single women in Italy, Australia, and England in the matter of a few weeks.

Says Davis, 38, who took a job in Kansas after losing her job in Chicago, "I thought I was going to die when I first moved to the small town where I live. There are days when I feel like the last single woman in the world. And it's so frustrating knowing that it's because of where I live. I certainly never felt that way in Chicago, where I hung around single people all the time. Thank God for the Internet is all I can say. I not only e-mail with my friends back home, but I've also met several Internet friends from forums for single women who feel like I do. Plus, clicking on sites for single women reminds me that there are so many single women out there like me—and I'm normal."

I found this posting from an anonymous contributor on a blog site: "I spent the majority of my single, twentysomething years living and attempting to date in and around a small town (pop. 7,000). Were it not for online dating, I'd have been screwed. You run through the eligible guys pretty quickly in a town that small . . . and for me, I'd grown up with most of them."

Expand your horizons—literally.

If you are within a couple hours of a city, make sure you get yourself there at least once a month to remind yourself there are real live women your age roaming around without a gold band on their finger. Plus, getting to an art museum, chic boutique, or ethnic restaurant will keep your brain expanding and your creativity flowing—and remind you there is a bigger world out there where your relationship status doesn't matter so much.

"I lived in a small town in Maryland for a while because of a job that was too good to pass up," said one single 26-year-old. "But I felt like a total leper being single, and there was no one to go out with on weekends because everyone stayed in with their families. I was miserable and my only savior was taking a train into D.C. on Saturdays. I loved being in a swell of people, with all these options, and seeing all these women walking around independently and doing their thing. It helped me last one more full year before I finally moved back to New England."

If there's no city nearby, make a point of walking through another town that's close by. You might not have a cultural extravaganza, but just walking around somewhere new, seeing new sights and new faces, can feed your soul. At the very least it will be a chance to get away from that one extra nosy neighbor who always wants to tell you about which community members recently became available. Of course, the other thing is that going to a town even smaller than yours will give you the perspective of seeing your own town in a new way. It's all relative, right?

 ## In case of emergency: Take the first flight out when necessary.

Keep at least enough cash in your savings account to purchase a last-minute flight if you're feeling closed in at home. Some of the best websites to check for last-minute deals include Travelzoo, Expedia, Kayak, and Travelocity. You won't believe the mental replenishing that can come out of having a ticket on your desk and knowing you'll be exploring a new locale soon. Take plenty of photos during your trip to remind yourself to do this again in the not-too-distant future. If you're broke (or saving money so you can get out of this place once and for all), rent a slew of international films that will make you feel like you're on vacation. To get you started, try *Out of Africa*, *Roman Holiday*, *Muriel's Wedding* (set in Australia), and *Amelie* (set in Paris).

$ BITE THE BULLET, GET LIFE INSURANCE

Perhaps you have enough on your plate, dealing with being single in a wedding-obsessed community. But there is something you should do if you don't have health insurance while you're in this location. Get a life insurance policy. A lot of single women without kids skip it, thinking why bother. The reason is that if you don't, your family is going to get stuck paying off your school loans and any debts you might have. No matter how aggravated you may be with your brother right now, do you really want to saddle him with your debt? Bite the bullet and get a policy—while you're young and healthy; you'll get reduced premiums and can lock in a fixed rate. Martin Brown, columnist for Single Minded Women (www.singlemindedwomen.com), says that an added bonus is that the cash value of your insurance policy can be used to secure loans.

TOP 5 CITIES TO BE SINGLE (ACCORDING TO *FORBES*, 2009)

If you're considering moving to (or even just visiting) a more single-friendly city, check out this list from *Forbes* that ranked forty of the largest continental U.S. urban areas in seven different categories: coolness, cost of living alone, culture, job growth, online dating, nightlife, and number of singles. (I've included a travel suggestion for each city.)

1. New York (Amble through the funky art galleries of SoHo, rain or shine.)
2. Boston (Enjoy a relaxing ride on the famous swan boats of the Boston Public Garden.)
3. Chicago (Take a Segway tour around the city to check out the inspiring architecture.)
4. Seattle (Pump up your adrenaline with a nighttime ghost tour through Pike Place Market.)
5. Washington, D.C. (Stroll the gorgeous gardens and monuments between the Capitol and the Lincoln Memorial.)

REMINDER CHECKLIST

1. Tune in to your inner voice: Does it make sense for you to stay put?
2. Write it down: What are the pros and cons of living in your community?

3. Make your escape plan . . . just in case. Knowing there is an out is sometimes all you need to not feel stuck.

4. Write it down: Where can you imagine relocating?

5. Make like a horror movie character and "get out of the house." Don't get lured by the comforts of home; you need to be with real people.

6. Widen your search past town boundaries. Appreciate that in some ways it might be easier dating in a small town.

7. Go scouting for townfolk. Make it your mission to socialize and gain a few acquaintances.

8. Get off the defensive. Help people in town better understand your circumstances instead of assuming they're criticizing you.

9. Shake up your perspective. Remember that the "marrieds" don't necessarily have it easier than you do.

10. Schedule the Mom talk. Let her know how tiring it is being the outcast.

11. Log on to the Internet and connect with singles. There are millions of singles around the world available for chatting on the World Wide Web.

12. Expand your horizons. Change the scenery in order to change your outlook.

13. In case of emergency: Take the first flight out when necessary.

9

The Ritual Reinventor

Definition: You want to get hitched but know that would require an unpopular overhaul of what the wedding and marriage look like.

Pop Quiz

If your office had a yearbook, the caption under your name would say:

A   "Best team player."
B   "Most likely to march to the beat of her own drum."
C   "Top team leader."

If you answered B, this chapter is for you.

DIANA'S STORY

Diana,* 41, knew she would be a women's-studies major by junior high school. "It was not surprising given that my dad dumped my mother when I was eight, and I had to take care of my sister while my mom tried to recover." Diana vowed that something like this was never going to happen to her. "I was going to be strong, make my own money, and never get into a position like my mom," she said. Diana railed against marriage to anyone who would listen and developed a support network of girlfriends who felt the same.

But things changed when Diana met Evan years later at a pro-choice rally. He asked to borrow a pen for a petition, and sparks flew. "We went from talking about the rally to sharing stories with each other I never thought I'd tell anyone," she said. "He was so kind and gentle; I'd never met a guy like him." The two started dating exclusively and then one night Evan proposed over dinner. Diana said no, that she was committed to him but did not believe in marriage. He agreed to try an unconventional route, but lately Diana has started to fantasize about a wedding surrounded by family and friends. She worries, however, that by marrying she would be "selling out."

Stage of Singlehood

You never expected in a million years to even consider planning a wedding for yourself. For the longest time, you thought you'd create your own road map and forgo marriage, but now you've met someone you want to spend your life with and are actually considering marrying him. *Marrying* him! Part of you, like Dina, feels that getting hitched now would be selling yourself out. Maybe you detest the idea of "following the crowd" and becoming part of the masses. Or as a feminist you are turned off by the idea of having someone "give you away." Perhaps you always considered monogamy archaic and impractical. But now, here you are dreaming of weddings, honeymoon destinations, and even (oddly enough) cake toppers. The old you and the new you seem to be at odds, and you need peace between the two.

The Great News

First of all, you are allowed to change your mind about opting to marry and shouldn't feel guilty about it at all. You know what works for you, and if it changes over the years, that's normal. People amend their wish lists all the time. If you're suddenly drawn to the idea of a traditional wedding (even a full-on bridal party), there is nothing wrong with that. You have not betrayed yourself or anyone else; you had a change of heart. This chapter will help you feel more secure in your new feelings and help you deflect the ribbing and provoking comments that are sure to come your way.

If the idea of a traditional wedding is so not you (but you are considering a different kind of wedding and marriage), this chapter will give you suggestions and tips for creating a ceremony that reflects your unconventional attitudes. Weddings don't have to include taffeta dresses, garter belts, and tossing the bouquet to a group of humiliated singles. More and more women today are reinventing their own rituals. Who says a wedding and marriage have to be anything other than what you and your partner decide? If you are willing to be brave and bold, you and your guy can create—and even showcase—a marriage that fully supports your modern beliefs and attitudes. In this chapter you'll find steps to help you think through what that could look like.

SHIFT YOUR THINKING

Old messages have to go.

It may be that your thoughts keep flipping back and forth: "I want to marry this guy!" . . . "No, marriage is wrong." . . . "It's different with this guy." . . . "Yeah, but that will all change the second we slip a gold band on our fingers." . . . "But I want the gold band!" . . . You can drive yourself crazy with all the dueling sentiments. Add to that the voices of some of your friends who scoff at marriage, along with others who implore you to bite the bullet and marry already . . . and it's no wonder your brain is full of chaos.

To figure out what is truly best for you right now, it's essential to clear your mind of old messages and lingering expectations. Forget about the parents gunning for you to wear the white gown. Never mind your friends who compare marriage to a lifetime in shackles. Let go of what you told yourself back in the day about weddings and what kind of life you pictured for your future. None of these things matter; you need to decide what works for you *now*.

By the way, plenty of women—including feminist poster child (scratch, make that poster woman) Gloria Steinem, who got hitched at age sixty-six—have gone on to change their mind about marriage and wed their partner. For these brides, it is a matter of figuring how to create a ceremony and lifestyle that reflects their personal beliefs and values. Sure, introducing new rituals means some guests may roll their eyes, but who cares? As a freethinker, you're used to that.

It's also imperative to remove all the "noise" of colleagues, friends, mothers, grandmothers, and other outside commentators who insist they know what's best for you ("You must go with a summer wedding." "Bands are far better than deejays, trust me"). What your wedding and marriage look like has to be decided between you and your partner, and the first step to figuring this out is determining what feels right for *you*.

ACTION STEPS

 ### Tune in to your inner voice: How does the idea of getting married feel?

Take a deep breath, close your eyes, and ask yourself, "Setting aside all outside pressure, how do I feel about getting married?" There's a good chance if you tune out what everyone else has to say on the matter, the answer will rise up from somewhere inside of you—the honest answer. In addition to tuning in to your feelings, pay attention to how your body responds. When you think of the wedding, are you smiling or grimacing? Are your muscles clenched or relaxed? You will know the answer is right for you because you'll breathe easier and feel a sense of relief in the moment. Don't lose sight of that answer. Protect it, because it will lead you to where you are supposed to be.

Accept that your feelings may have changed.

Are you surprised by your answer? You may feel out of sorts but, again, you are allowed to have a change of heart—even a

180-degree change. It's normal and appropriate to shift your thinking based on new situations that arise in your life, new circumstances, and people you meet. If that wasn't true, we'd all still believe the tooth fairy was coming and that wearing braces was the worst thing that could happen to a person. No one can or should hold you accountable to old beliefs that no longer fit you. It's quite possible that "marriage" as a concept didn't work for you until you found this wonderful partner who wants the same things out of life that you do. Had you known this guy existed, maybe you never would have dismissed the idea of marriage in the first place.

Take Jacquie, 35, for example. Marriage was the last thing on her mind when she was younger, and she never once dreamt about a big white wedding as a girl. "My parents got divorced when I was ten, so I don't have a lot of memories before that on my thoughts about marriage," she said. "But I definitely remember being eleven or twelve and making a conscious decision that I was not going to be in the same situation that my mother was. She got divorced in her early thirties and was suddenly the single mom of two kids, as a result of my father's infidelity." Jacquie told herself again and again, "No matter what happens, I can always take care of myself." There was a good chance, she knew, she would never marry because she wouldn't risk being in that position. Then, destiny stepped in: she met and fell in love with Gabe, and saw what a relationship could look like with a decent, stable guy who made her feel safe. She can't imagine life without him. Will she marry him? "I don't know," she said, "I think so." What's important, she understands, is making a choice based on where she is *now* versus how she felt as a young girl when her father left.

Ellie Levenson, author of *The Noughtie Girl's Guide to Feminism*, grew up thinking, "We don't need to be married in society to have a valid relationship. Nobody stops couples living together, buying property together, or having children, regardless of marital status. I thought marriage was outdated and silly." Then years later, she too met a wonderful man, fell in love, and tied the knot. According to Ellie, "I remembered the words of a former colleague. She had told me, many times, as I railed against marriage, this nugget of truth: 'You won't want to get married until you meet the man you want to marry.'"

The point is not that you *should* change your mind about getting married, just that you're *allowed* to—and without feeling like you betrayed yourself. Besides, if you forgo marriage solely to stay consistent with your old beliefs, you're going to end up with big regrets.

Realize you're the same person regardless of a wedding.

Given the value you place on being a freethinker, it's important to remind yourself that getting married can't lessen or nix this quality. There is no moment during or after the ceremony when you morph into a traditional 1950s housewife and start fetching slippers for your husband. That doesn't mean women don't worry about it all the time, though.

Dana,* 29, told me, "I have always done things my own way and not cared what anyone thinks. I was the girl who wore army boots when the other girls wore ballet flats. I was reading physics books when other girls were reading Judy Blume books. I never, ever thought I would get married, but then I met a guy who 'got me,' and it just felt right. I knew I wanted to spend my life with him and I almost blew it by saying no to his marriage proposal." Dana told me the only reason she was going to say no was that being a wife didn't "fit her image" of herself. She didn't want to lose herself; eventually, however, she realized this was "about my life and not wanting to lose this amazing guy. I had to trust he wouldn't expect me to become a different person, which, of course, he didn't." She said they've been happily married for three years and she's "still the same weirdo as always."

Michelle, 34, worried she'd lose her independence: "The biggest challenge was my fear of being trapped. I'm fiercely independent and, frankly, for most of my twenties I imagined a future for myself of living all over the world, being the eccentric aunt to all my friends' kids who comes home every once in a while with exotic gifts and stories. I saw marriage as confining. Then, much to my chagrin, and like the total cliché, I found myself increasingly drawn to domesticity in my late twenties. For a few years now, this sense of some primal, uncontrollable biological clock has confused me because it has felt so conflicting. My now husband and I were engaged for six years!" After the two married, Michelle says they started figuring out how to create a marriage that allows them to retain their independence but also rely on each other. She still considers herself a strong feminist.

If you, too, fear losing your independent ways and/or equality in your relationship, take a step back and think about your relationship *now*. You have undoubtedly crafted a partnership that supports, even enhances, your beliefs and lifestyle. I'm guessing the guy you have chosen would actually freak out if you suddenly started playing needy girl to make him feel big and strong. He clearly did not fall in love with you for your codependent ways.

Neither a wedding nor a marriage can compromise your beliefs if you continue to define your own path; if anything, marriage should highlight your attitudes, not stifle them.

 ## Write it down: What quality do you fear losing if you marry?

Spend ten or fifteen minutes recording in your journal what you fear losing about yourself once you say "I do." It may be just one thing, it may be many; write whatever comes to mind. When you're done, look at your answer and ask yourself whether you can really picture losing this valuable piece of yourself, or whether it is inherently you. If it feels like you risk losing it, how can you prevent this from happening? What steps can you take?

Theo,* 27, did just that and realized she was scared of losing her identity as a feminist. "Here I was, this woman who had spent the last ten years traveling to D.C. from Boston to march for women's rights, writing letters to my senator to protect women's rights, and helping to fight for same-sex marriage in my state," she said. "When my boyfriend proposed, my first thought was, 'Yes!' But then I started worrying that I was going to be the little wife at home. He didn't think that, it was my own irrational fear. So I made a list of all the causes I've taken on and will keep taking on, and I look at that if I ever question losing this piece of me."

Give your vision of marriage a makeover.

As Betsy Stephenson, professor of economics at Wharton, reminds us, "If you go back to 1970, and ask college-educated women what they were looking for in a husband, they still said a good provider. And women ultimately don't say that anymore. What they more commonly say now is, 'Someone who gets me or someone I can connect with.'" And although many traditionalists believe that marriage is too confusing as the roles of husbands and wives become more equal and undifferentiated, Betsy says, "When we look at marital satisfaction data, we see that more educated women are getting more satisfaction out of their marriages. So in that sense, we might say their marriages are more successful."

It's not easy redefining marriage from scratch. But it might help, as Betsy pointed out, to realize that you're not alone in this. When you start getting nervous that marriage means you will be expected to play the traditional role of cook, cleaner, woman who runs all the errands, think again. Really examine and explore what a good marriage looks like to you, what it could look like, what your fears are, and what your hopes are.

Melissa, 29, has already decided. "My ideal marriage is to have a husband who supports me, and I support him. He has his own interests, I have mine. I can't be stuck in the house all day living my life through my children. I do believe I'll be a great mom, but my life isn't going to revolve around my children. I still have to go out and have my own interests, go golfing, spend a Saturday afternoon with the girls. You know, having coffee or heading to the beach with some friends. I just can't be one of those people who has no outside life."

Tanya, 40, said, "I knew that I did not want a marriage like my mother and my aunts had. They basically slaved over their husbands all night, in spite of the fact that they were working women by day. That made it much harder for me to get on board with marriage after my boyfriend proposed. I have spent the last year talking to friends who are married and happy. They have real partnerships with their husbands, with both people providing for each other. Now that I know this really exists, I'm starting to feel better about the idea of marriage."

Talk to other women who have taken the challenge to redefine their roles in marriage. If you don't know any personally, ask your friends and peers to talk to their network of people and find someone you can compare notes with. Just hearing other women tell you that it is possible to reinvent marriage on your own terms can be a relief and even inspiring. As a bonus, hearing how they did it—and how they dealt with judgmental commentary from others—can help you figure out some steps ahead of time. If they can do it, so can you.

Call upon your other half.

Don't lose sight of the fact that you have a partner to help you think through what a wedding and marriage might look like. If you're even considering becoming legally wed, open the discussion with your guy; hey, you might as well get used to figuring out how to work together on big complicated projects at the potential start of your marriage. Have you sat down and asked him what he is looking for in terms of your future together (assuming he even wants one) and how *he* sees the roles you'll take on? What are his expectations about raising a child together if you have one? Hopefully, if you are at a place of considering marriage, you have already been discussing these topics along the way, but you might want to take it up a notch and make sure you're on the same page.

Assuming that goes well, it may be time to imagine together

what a wedding might look like that reflects you as a couple. Maybe you hate the whole idea of a bachelorette party and making your friends suffer through a bridal shower. Then lose the traditions (they are not set in stone). Maybe there are certain rituals he can do without. Maybe he loves the idea of a bachelor party, maybe he detests it. Ask him. Can you picture the details of a wedding you would both feel good about? If not, there are a lot of novel ideas out there from women who were in exactly the same position and created a ceremony that became a perfect expression of their commitment. Here's what some of them said:

"For me, the worst part of a wedding is the idea of trying on dozens of poofy white dresses in some bridal shop, and looking the same as every other woman who is getting married. It's supposed to be a 'special' day. How special can it be if every bride looks the same? Plus, the whole idea of a white dress expressing purity just made me laugh. I'm not that pure. So I found a comfortable dress that was edgy like me, and wore a pair of flats on my feet. I just shrugged when people told me I had to wear heels."

"I talked to my now-husband about the fact that I hated the idea of everyone staring at me while my father 'gave me away.' It just felt so against how I live my life, which is as a strong, fierce woman. He told me he couldn't picture it, either, so we talked it out and decided that we would walk down the aisle together. It was really empowering actually, and made me feel even more certain that he was the right man for me. I knew he would hear me out and support me throughout my life, and we'd be a team."

"My fiancé and I approached the wedding as a truly united front. I came up with some unconventional ideas, like having a vegetarian buffet with sustainable foods. He came up with his own ideas, like asking people to donate to charities instead of giving gifts. It felt like 'us.' Anytime we were confronted with 'Usually how it's done . . .' or 'The bride ordinarily . . .' one of us would interrupt with, 'Excuse me, but this is our wedding, and *we* want . . .'"

Know that you don't have to participate in any of the established wedding rituals you've grown up seeing; your big day is a blank slate. Tell your boyfriend that you want to feel like the day really reflects who you are as a couple. Don't assume because you discussed your wedding once or twice, you're on the same page. It's a conversation that should continue to be revisited. If you are looking for more ways to create an indie wedding, check out the sidebar "7 More Ideas for a Modern Wedding."

Prepare to lose acquaintances.

Hopefully, upon seeing your happiness, most friends will be excited for you. There may be old comrades-in-arms, however, who disapprove of your wedding announcement. They would never in a hundred years even consider matrimony and have been extremely vocal about this. That's fine, as long as they support *your* plans. They can be disappointed that you are opting for a mainstream lifestyle, but also be glad you are happy (these are not mutually exclusive). If, on the other hand, they keep insisting in subtle or obvious ways that you are acting like a traitor by joining the masses, it may be time to part ways. They are not going to support you and that's a problem, so see it for what it is: a relationship that was good for you during a specific window of time in your life but no longer.

Jessica Valenti, founder of the blog Feministing.com, said that when she and her husband Andrew got married, most of her feminist readers had hearty congratulations to give. Others, however, said she was no longer helping take down the patriarchy. In an article called "My Big Feminist Wedding" in *The Guardian*, Jessica said that "Kathryn Lopez of the conservative publication *National Review* wrote a post entitled 'You've Never Met a Bridezilla Like a Feminist Bridezilla,' mocking my attempts to subvert traditional wedding standards." Ultimately, Jessica has to ignore the negative commentary and focus on heading into a marriage of two equals.

"I have a friend," one bride told me, "who said she's boycotting my wedding because she is so against wedding ceremonies, but she still wants to be my friend. I don't know how I feel about that. I am making a choice that is right for me and her political agenda won't allow her to be happy for me. I don't know that I can just shove aside the fact that she is intentionally missing one of the biggest days of my life."

In the heat of the moment, these conflicts can get ugly. It's one thing when your friend has differing political views and another when she won't support your life decision because of her views. But remember that friends aren't required to share all of the same beliefs. Many a Republican woman can enjoy ladies' night out with her Democratic sisters. Vegetarians who are repulsed by meat can still hang out with burger-loving friends. Your friends can disagree on whether weddings are acts of celebration or torture but, as friends, they should want you to do what feels right for you. Mind you, they shouldn't be forced to catch the bouquet at your wedding or pay for an overly expensive bridesmaid dress, but they should at the very least be there for you with a smile on their face on the big day.

Have a response to
"I *knew* you'd get married!"

If you do decide to get hitched, prepare for certain people to rub your face in it. "Sooooo," they will accuse, "I knew you'd change your mind about marriage!" or offer smugly, "Huh! I thought you didn't *do* weddings," or "Boy, for someone who was so totally against weddings, I was pretty surprised to hear you changed your mind." The basic goal of all these comments is to prove how absolutely right they were and how wrong you were. It's irritating, even infuriating.

But in the bigger picture, so what?

You can allow yourself to get agitated and spend your time dwelling in how obnoxious these know-it-alls are. But, in the end, who really cares whether they think they've been right and you've been wrong? It only matters if you allow it to matter. If you get flustered and upset, they win the upper hand and will go on driving you crazy, which is the last thing you need as you step into this next phase of your life. Instead, pay no attention when they start blathering about how they knew you'd end up in the white dress. You can even smile and say without anger, "I know. Who knew there'd be a [name of your guy]?" or "Yep, I changed my mind." You basically give them no satisfaction by remaining neutral and they move on. End of story.

Congratulate yourself for following through on what's right for you and for not getting sidetracked by what anyone else thinks. You're staying true to your own needs, and none of these people can take that away.

Schedule the Mom talk: Share your unique wedding vision with her.

If the traditional, by-the-book wedding is not for you, then you may find yourself in plenty of unnerving negotiations with your mom. Let's face it, she may have been looking forward to your wedding day since you were a little girl, and long held her own idea of how it would go. Unfortunately, it looks nothing like the vision in your own head.

Inform your mother way ahead of time that your wedding is not going to look like the fantasy in her mind. Hey, maybe she'll be so surprised and elated that you're considering marrying at all, that she'll take what she can get. But don't be surprised if she starts talking to you about what kind of canapés will be served, what your bridesmaids will wear, and whether you are going to go with a tulle or a simple straight-line dress. You'll have to set the woman straight, but kindly.

Take her to lunch so you're on neutral territory, and open with, "Mom, I want to talk to you about my wedding. There are going to be a lot of nontraditional elements to it and I want to tell you about it so there are no huge surprises." Assure her that you and your fiancé have worked on this wedding plan together and are completely in sync with each other. Then if she says, "How can you even think of not having a gift registry?" you can reply, "We talked about it and decided together that it's not for us."

One hint though. It will help if you can give your mom a task or two and let her have free reign with it. Maybe she can be in charge of flowers. In the scope of things, does it really matter whether there are daffodils or petunias on your wedding day? Letting Mom be in charge of the floral display is an easy way to empower her and make her feel included that's at no great expense to you.

In case of emergency:
Take it from *Ms.* . . .

If you're afraid that getting married makes you less of yourself, write down this item from *Ms.* magazine's "Who Wants to Marry a Feminist?" by Lisa Miya-Jervis. "To reject marriage simply because of its history is to give in to that history; to argue against marriage by saying that a wife's identity is necessarily subsumed by her husband's is to do nothing more than second the notion." Read it to yourself if and when you start to question whether marriage gets in the way of feminism.

$ RAISE MONEY WHILE CELEBRATING YOUR DIFFERENCES

If you do decide to get married and already own your own blender, towels, and new dishes, consider asking friends and family to make a donation to a cause they believe in instead of spending the money on a gift for you. Allowing everyone to pick their own causes and charities shows that you respect the choices they make for themselves. How perfect given that this is just what you want from them at your wedding—respect and an open mind. You may want to provide a page of Web links to the most mainstream charities for those you know will have an impossible time making a choice. The point is to empower guests, not make them crazy. Also, don't get distressed if some relatives give you crystal vases and fruit bowls instead of donating money. They couldn't help themselves (and now you have a treasure to regift).

7 MORE IDEAS FOR A MODERN WEDDING

1. Instead of having Daddy "give you away," ask both parents to walk you down the aisle, take yourself down, or walk with your soon-to-be hubby.
2. Skip the dreaded bouquet toss for single women.
3. Pay for the wedding instead of having your parents foot the bill. That way, you won't get roped into creating their vision of a wedding.
4. Ditch the phrase "honor and obey" from your vows, and create a new set of commitments for the two of you.
5. Replace "maid of honor" with "woman of honor," and come up with a better, cooler name than "bridesmaids."
6. Have your wedding outside so it won't feel institutional.
7. Elope.

REMINDER CHECKLIST

1. Tune in to your inner voice: How does the idea of getting married feel?

2. Accept that your feelings may have changed. You do not have to defend your shift in attitude, even if you're experiencing a 180-degree change.

3. Take back your power. Standing at the altar doesn't diminish your freethinker status.

4. Write it down: What quality do you fear losing if you marry?

5. Give your vision of marriage a makeover. Realize you are one of many women today changing the look of marriage.

6. Call upon your other half. Get on the same page with your man about what your actual marriage would look like so there are no surprises.

7. Prepare to lose acquaintances. Friends who can't support your choice may no longer deserve a spot on your friendship list.

8. Have a response to "I *knew* you'd get married!" Don't allow others' smugness to get in the way of your happiness.

9. Schedule the Mom talk. Tell your mother that you are interested in having a wedding, but not the one she dreamt for you.

10. In case of emergency: Take it from Ms....

PART FOUR

Navigating a Marriage-Obsessed Culture

♥

Time-out, people. Who decided this was
a race, and what's the *&#^*ing* rush?

The Someday Mom

Definition: You wish there was a snooze button on your biological clock so you wouldn't feel so pressured.

Pop Quiz

If a psychic told you that you'd have a baby in the next three years, you'd:

A   Consider using three forms of birth control.

B   Start talking to friends who have babies if you need advice.

C   Sort through paint samples for the walls of your baby's nursery.

If you answered B or C, this chapter is for you.

CHERYL'S STORY

Cheryl, 37, was "always thinking about my biological clock—it's that sound that just never goes away, especially when you are lying in bed at night." It's especially frustrating for Cheryl when she sees her friends playing with their children and during family get-togethers when she feels like she's let down her mom. Cheryl says she finally decided to do something about it when she realized that she was remaining in relationships with men who she knew were wrong for her. She admitted, "I would think, 'Well, I could live with that. He seems like he could be a good father or a good husband. Maybe he isn't passionate or doesn't make as much money as I do, or maybe we'll have a problem in this area of our relationship, but I could probably make it work.'"

Understanding how close she was to settling for the wrong guy, Cheryl decided to freeze her eggs at a fertility clinic. It cost thousands of dollars and the research was overwhelming, as were the daily shots of hormones she had to inject herself with. "I know that the odds for freezing one's eggs successfully are pretty low," Cheryl said, "but it was worth it for me because it allows me to make better dating choices and I feel far less likely to settle for some guy just because of my ticking clock."

Stage of Singlehood

There are moments when you hear your biological clock ticking like something out of Edgar Allan Poe's "The Tell-Tale Heart." And you'd like it to *pipe down* already. Whether you have long dreamt of having a baby or not, you don't like this constant and nagging reminder that your eggs have a shelf life and they're quickly approaching expiration. Nor is it helpful that some people, too many to count, keep pointing it out. *Oh, really? I'm not getting any younger?* I mean, what are you supposed to do about that fact? Get knocked up by a stranger because time is running out? You're not ready to be a mom right now. Either you're waiting to find a husband first, or you want to parent a child but you're just not there yet. *So could somebody stop that ticking, please?!*

The Great News

If you're reading this chapter, it's likely you've been (a) experiencing a whole lot of pressure to get going on the baby front, (b) worrying about how much time is left on your clock, or (c) feeling disappointed because you desperately wanted a child by now. With each passing year, the frenzy picks up and it's getting harder to picture how this is all going to play out. But the positive news is that this chapter will help you think calmly through whether you really do want a baby, what conditions you'd need to have in place, and how to make peace with the steps you do or do not take. And, yes, it is possible to make peace.

Whether you want to have a child now or down the road, you'll find ideas and strategies in this chapter that you can use starting today (that don't include tossing your birth control out the window). There are no easy answers or guarantees you'll have a baby the old-fashioned way, but you can take control of the situation and know you're making all the best decisions you can for yourself.

SHIFT YOUR THINKING

Look your ticking clock full in its clock face.

Many of the women I interviewed hadn't put much thought into whether they would have a baby on their own if they didn't meet a partner before age forty, or how they would deal with their decreasing fertility. These women, so used to researching everything from where to invest their money to how to track down the perfect cappuccino, had put little or no time into thinking through their own options for having a baby.

It's not that they forgot or didn't see it as important; it's that the idea of getting pregnant and becoming a mother felt so overwhelming that it was easier to just ignore it and hope things worked out for the best. Unfortunately, this is a really bad plan if you think you might want to have a child. The reality is your biological clock does not care about your good intentions or whether you are a lovely person. The quality and quantity of your eggs *is* decreasing each year, and you can't afford to pretend this isn't true.

If you're thinking "Shut up, shut up, shut up!" I get it, believe me. But my point is not to freak you out; it's to get you thinking about this right now so you can sit in the driver's seat rather than relying on destiny for a major life decision. You don't have to have the answers right now for the exact conditions (husband, no husband, certain salary, work schedule, etc.) you would need in order to have a baby. You do, however, need to realize that if you avoid addressing the issue because dealing with it is too painful, then you have essentially made a decision already for "no baby." And this decision to *not deal* may leave you deeply regretful because it will have been made without your intention. There is no right answer when it comes to whether you *should* try to get pregnant, or when or how. But it is crucial to your well-being that you stay conscious about what choices you are prepared to take.

ACTION ITEMS

 **Tune in to your inner voice:
Do you *really* want to have a baby?**

Spend a few quiet minutes asking yourself whether it's the baby you desire or ending the pressure to become a mother.

Realize it's okay to feel uncertain.

There are definitely women who seem born to be moms, fantasizing about their future children every chance they get. They can't help but sigh longingly whenever they see little girl dresses or wee toddler shoes. But plenty of other women go back and forth on the idea, leaning toward kids but also leaving room for the possibility of not having them. It's just not clear cut. If the latter sounds more like you, this uncertainty may be something you learn to tolerate until you feel more sure one way or the other.

Certainly some people believe that if you are on the fence about having babies while in your thirties, you should go ahead and take the maternal plunge. They say you can figure out how to make the rest of your life work—the career, a relationship—as you go, but you get only one window of opportunity to get pregnant and have the baby. I don't know about that. There's no question that raising a child takes an extraordinary amount of hard work and responsibility; taking on motherhood mainly out of fear (so you won't miss the window) feels like a recipe for resentment and potential disaster. Ultimately, I think it makes the most sense to look at where you are right now and what works for you given your *current* situation. Your feelings may change over time—no to a baby right now, possibly yes to a baby someday.

As Rachael, a 37-year-old single writer in New York City, said, "Somebody once said to me nature's cruel joke on women is that we can't have children forever. And you know, it's sort of true. I find myself feeling this fear of 'Oh, my God, I'm not going to be able to procreate, which is what we're put on this earth to do.' And then I find myself getting furious at feminism, saying damn, you know, you told me to do all these things, and I've gotten to this point. I took the right steps and I've gotten to a place now where I'm so incredibly fulfilled by my career and my life, but you know, I haven't had a child yet!" She said she wonders sometimes what would happen if she had had a baby earlier, but she knows she just wasn't ready.

Cindy Guidry, 45, the author of *The Last Single Woman in America,* told me, "I spent much of my thirties collecting little baby items for the day when I'd have a kid of my own. But at some point, I ran out of time, and I realized it wasn't going to happen. So now I have started giving those items to other new moms for gifts." For her, being in her late thirties was the hardest time of being single because she felt a certain desperation to be a mom, but now that it's not so possible the old-fashioned way, she's finding it easier to move on.

Allow yourself to feel frustration.

It's painful knowing you want to have a child and feeling emotionally ready in many ways, but understanding the timing isn't right. The clock is ticking and there are no prospects on the horizon. A lot of women find it maddening that they did everything right: they got college degrees, landed great jobs, became self-sufficient, and set up fine lives for themselves. And now this major next step that they want so badly is just out of their reach, and there is nothing they can do. It doesn't help to keep your frustration bottled in if you're feeling this way. Vent it, so you can then do something about it.

Here are some quotes from women I interviewed:

"It's so unfair. I was the one who did everything right. I got a great job, made a lot of money so I could support a kid, had safe, protected sex so there wouldn't be accidents, made sure I was ready physically and financially, and now I find out that the only way I'm going to be able to have kids is to pay thousands of dollars and go through these freaky invasive procedures."

"I have stuck countless needles in my body as I go through in vitro fertilization and soon I will have my eggs harvested while I am unconscious at some clinic, all in the hopes that this may lead to a pregnancy. I mean, how surreal is this? How did I get here?"

"I don't know if I'll have a baby. I don't feel like I necessarily have to have a baby to feel like a complete person or to be really happy. But I don't like that the choice is being taken away from me. I'm a strong, smart, independent woman who's worked hard to get where I am, and I hate having to cave in to a ticking clock."

"My best friend got pregnant recently and I couldn't deal with it. I was so jealous, and our friendship deeply suffered from it."

Venting isn't going to create a baby, but it is the first step to realizing how important this is to you so you can concentrate on taking active steps toward motherhood.

Let yourself off the hook.

Some of the women I talked to about their biological clock said they do have regrets. They admitted to me that if they knew they would be in this position—at the mercy of their biological clocks—they would have had a baby in their late twenties or early thirties with a male friend or an ex.

Plenty said they don't know what they'd do different—maybe nothing—but it's just painful to know your fertility window is closing every year. They were wondering all the time if they should be doing more: starting the paperwork for an adoption, freezing their eggs, looking into purchasing vials of sperm, *something*.

These are complicated issues and it would be condescending to offer some pat answer or tell you everything works out for the best. These kinds of huge decisions come with all sorts of mixed emotions, and you might feel happy you didn't rush into motherhood on some days and deeply regretful the next. That's okay, and it's normal. It doesn't mean you've done anything wrong. What's not healthy, however, is dwelling in it or beating yourself up for not having a baby already. Putting your energy on blaming yourself is bad for your psyche and is not going to bring a baby into your life.

Know that you made decisions that worked best for you at the time. What else could you do? You didn't have hindsight or a crystal ball, so you made the very best choices you could. Be gentle with yourself if you have days of sadness or longing, as you would be to a best friend in the same situation. If you find you are thinking obsessively about your past choices, talk to an expert— a therapist, clergy member, or someone from another support system. It's okay to experience disappointment, but you need to get help if you find you are are depressed and unable to move forward with your life.

 ## Write it down: What are your requirements?

Write in your journal for twenty minutes or so the answer to the question "What are the biggest conditions I would need to have in place to consider having a baby?" Don't censor or judge your answers, just start writing. You might ask yourself:

- Do I need to have a partner, or would I have one alone?
- Is there a certain amount of money I would need in the bank?
- What kind of support system would I need to lock in place?
- Would I use artificial means (sperm donation, surrogacy, donor eggs, etc.)?
- Would I be willing to consider adoption?

The women I interviewed had varied ideas and requirements that would have to be set in place when it came to raising a child. Here are some of their thoughts:

Susannah, 38, said, "It's not like I'm eighteen with this dreamy idea of what it's like to be a mommy, because I have no clue. I have several good friends who are moms and they are really open with me about how hard it is and how often they want to run away and just take a break—and those are happy moms who don't regret it. Those are also moms with husbands who really pitch in. So, yes, I do want to be a mom really badly but if I can't find a husband, do I want to do this on my own?"

Kristine, a 37-year-old, said, "Yes, I could have a baby on my own and pay for the hospital bills. But could I pay for the care of this child for eighteen years? Plus, I like to think that my parents would be there to help out if I had a baby on my own, but let's face it, they're getting older and older and at some point they won't be able to help. Plus, it's likely that there will be a point when I have to take care of them, which could be time-consuming and expensive, so where does that leave me in terms of trying to parent as a single person?"

More than a few women told me they hope to become mothers in their late thirties or early forties but are not willing to do anything invasive to their bodies, like using hormones or investing in artificial reproductive techniques. One single woman told me, "If it's meant to be, it's meant to be. I am not going to mess with my body to make it happen." Another interviewee said, "There's something creepy about using science to change your body makeup so you can have a child. It's much more likely I'd adopt." Another said, "There's a reason Mother Nature makes it hard for women to have babies past a certain age. Maybe we're not supposed to."

Plenty of women told me that they think it makes far more sense to have babies later in life than to give birth in their twenties. They argue that it's only after hitting thirty that many women are *able* to take care of kids financially, can rely on the wisdom they earned from real-life experiences, and are no longer obsessed with ambition and climbing the ladder because they have done that already. For many of these women, it's a blessing that there are continually more advancements in reproductive technology.

Certainly the number of college-educated single mothers is on the rise. According to Lucie Schmidt, economist at Williams College: in 1960 unmarried mothers accounted for 5 percent of births in the United States; that number today is 40 percent—and increasing numbers of those are college-educated and over the age of thirty. A headline in *The Washington Post* on May 6, 2010, reported that "More Children Are Being Born to Women Over 35 Than to Teens, PEW Study Finds." Because of this dramatic rise, there are more resources for single moms by choice than ever. A quick Google search brings up scores of blogs for single moms by choice, countless parenting books, websites full of educational and social resources, chat rooms for single moms who want to talk about their experiences or set up local community get-togethers. There are single-moms-by-choice discussion groups, reading guides, lectures, and workshops. No one is suggesting it is anything close to easy, but there has certainly never been a better time to be a single mom in terms of support.

Lastly, you may be clear on whether you want a baby and how far you'd go to have one. Or, like a lot of women, you might feel hazy and change your mind depending on the day. That's okay. So long as you continue getting educated and updated about your fertility and tuning in to your inner voice to see whether your feelings change, you can be confident that the decision to have a baby or not will be your *decision* and not something that happens arbitrarily to you. You might not be able to slow down your biological clock, but exploring where you stand will turn down the volume of the ticking and, likely, bring peace of mind.

Beat your doctor to the punch.

Talk to your doctor as soon as possible and ask him/her point-blank about your fertility. According to Dr. Glade Curtis, M.D., author of *Pregnancy After 35*: "When it comes to a woman's fertility after 30, it is not a precipitous drop at a certain age, but more a gradual decline." But, that said, "the longer you put off the decision, the more your chances of success will go down."

So do not assume everything is fine and your eggs are in perfect condition because the issue hasn't been raised by your doctor. He or she may have selfish reasons for avoiding the fertility questions. According to Dr. Kimberly Thornton, an endocrinologist at Boston IVF, "many doctors do not want to bring up the topic of fertility during office visits because they don't want to come across as judgmental or invasive. So rather than risk upsetting the patient or worrying her, they wait for the patient to bring it up with them."

Kerry, 45, recalled, "When I was forty, I went for my annual gynecological checkup. I'd recently moved, so it was a new doctor. After my checkup, while still lying down, my doctor loomed over me and asked me if I wanted to have children. I was about to reply when my doctor said, 'You've got two years at best, probably one. Your time is running out, so if you want them it needs to be now.' I was stunned."

This is obviously not the way you want to begin a conversation about your fertility options. Here's the bottom line: It's not your doctor who is going to have to live with the consequences of you having a baby or not; it's you. So bring it up at your next appointment, or schedule one now with your doctor specifically to discuss your options. If you sense that your doctor is out of his or her element (uncomfortable discussing the issue, or uneducated about the latest techniques available), find a fertility specialist and make an appointment. Being armed with reliable information is the most important step toward your decision making.

Know your (real) alternatives.

Do not get deluded by pregnant TV and film stars over age forty that grace the cover of Hollywood celebrity magazines. Many women told me they weren't worried about their fertility because "if Julia Roberts and Halle Berry can get pregnant, so can I." But we have no idea how celebrities on magazine covers got pregnant or how many thousands of dollars they invested into making that happen. What we do know is that many women in their late thirties and older are using donor eggs. "But my aunt's friend's sister has a baby at forty-four," you may be thinking. That's right. There are women who do get pregnant naturally past the age of forty, and that could indeed be you. But if we're looking at statistics, it's not likely. By the time you hit age forty, you have a less than five percent chance every month of getting pregnant naturally. You certainly should not bank on these low odds.

Research what options are available to you in reproductive technology, and keep a list of the pros/cons of each technique. Several women I interviewed had heard of "egg freezing" and figured they'd try that if more years passed and they still hadn't found a partner to be the father. What most of them didn't realize is that the success rates are quite low right now (somewhere around 25 percent for women in their late thirties) and the cost is quite high, typically $10,000 to $15,000 per cycle with a good chance you'll need to go through more than one cycle. This doesn't mean that women shouldn't freeze their eggs, but they should do their homework and understand what the process looks like before deciding this is their backup plan.

The same is true for all assisted reproductive technology. Take note of what technologies are new on the horizon so you can check back for advancements in the future. The field of reproductive technology is changing at dramatic rates as the demand grows.

Some websites that may be helpful with your research:

- American Society for Reproductive Medicine (www.asrm .org): a multidisciplinary organization dedicated to the advancement of the art, science, and practice of reproductive medicine
- The National Infertility Center (www.resolve.org): a nonprofit organization with the only established, nationwide network mandated to promote reproductive health
- Fertility Authority (www.fertilityauthority.com): a source for fertility information, from diagnosis to resolution

Find out where your guy stands.

There were plenty of single women I interviewed in their early to midthirties who were in the early stages of a relationship with a man who said he wasn't ready for kids anytime soon. Many of these women knew they wanted babies and weren't getting any younger, and they worried about "losing" their fertile years to a guy who wouldn't end up being *the* guy. They wanted to know whether they should stay in the relationship and hope the guy would change his tune eventually, or bail now.

Said Tara,* 34, who has been with her boyfriend for five months, said, "I love him, I totally trust him, and this is the healthiest relationship I've ever had. But he's not sure whether he wants to have kids and I don't know if I want to keep investing in this relationship if he doesn't, so what am I supposed to do?"

The first step, assuming you want to have babies in the next couple of years, is to ask your man what he thinks about having kids and when. I'm not talking about bringing it up on the first date (or even the first few dates), but as you realize you're considering him as a partner. You don't have to make a huge dramatic deal of it. Just tell him calmly, "I want to be clear about what we see for ourselves. I know that I want to have babies in the next couple of years, and I hope that's something you want as well. But if it's not, then I'd rather know earlier rather than later." Then listen to his answer. What does he say, and how does he say it? Does he hem and haw, or is he straightforward? Does his answer seem genuine, or is he trying to buy time by being purposefully vague? How do you feel about his answer? Are you clear on where he stands? You may be thinking right now, "How am I supposed to know?" But chances are you do know, and the real question is whether you are prepared to deal with it.

There's no black-and-white answer for whether you should stay with your boyfriend (if he's not certain about wanting to parent), because it depends on how much you value your relationship and how strongly you feel about having a baby. If the answer is, "I want babies yesterday," then it matters how ready your guy is and how long it will take him to have an answer if he is on the fence.

When I asked Tara how she'd feel if she broke up with her boyfriend today, she said, "I'm not ready to break up!" She also told me that finding the right partner is much more important to her than having a baby—though she'd prefer both. So that's where she is *right now*. Instead of parting ways or giving him a deadline, she plans to enjoy her relationship with him and knows there might come a day when she will change her mind and walk away. She is choosing to stay mindful rather than racing out of the relationship before she is ready and potentially regretting it.

If your boyfriend (like Tara's) tells you he's not sure about having kids, you will have to make a point of being extra in touch with how you feel as you weigh your options. Can you give him more time without feeling like he's wasting your time? Whatever you do, don't give him an ultimatum ("If you can't commit to wanting to be a father in two months, we're breaking up"). There's no faster way to kill a relationship than to tell someone they have to be ready to have a baby with you by a certain date. If you stay with him, check in with yourself regularly and pay attention to his words and his actions over the upcoming months. Is he trying to work the decision through, or is he stalling for time? Only you can decide how emotionally risky staying with him is. Keep listening to your inner voice and you'll know soon enough whether it makes sense to stick it out with him.

Silence the baby-obsessed.

Unfortunately, most of the single women I interviewed for the film told me that while there may be more single mothers by choice today, the pressure to have kids is as great as ever. One fortysomething told me, "It may be more common to wait or not have kids, but, believe me, there is still a definite stigma! You are made to feel like a monster." So you need a way to handle the people in your life who openly begrudge and denounce you for "letting your time slip away." They have no problem pointing out that "you're getting older," and "if you want to have a baby, you need to get cooking." For something so entirely personal, it's amazing how many people think they have the right to step in and tell you what you should be doing.

Some will tell you that you should look into adoption or find out more about having a baby on your own, maybe buy some vials of sperm as backup. They will have all sorts of ideas and want to know what specifically you're doing about having a baby and whether you're taking this seriously enough.

Jill, 34, said, "I'm a pediatrician, so I am always asked by my patients and their families if I have children. When I say that I do not, the follow-up question is always, 'Why?' I swear that one of these days I am going to just say that I am infertile . . . not the truth . . . that I just can't find a good man to knock me up."

Given that you may have to respond to personal, or downright offensive, questions and comments for a while, you need a response that sets the record straight while making it clear this is not up for discussion. It's best to keep it short, friendly, and direct when someone starts getting up in your face about not having a baby. It can be as simple as: "I love kids, but I'm not ready yet." When they say (and they will) something like, "You'd better hop to it, then!" you can restate, "As I said, I'm not ready yet." One fortysomething woman answers, "Well, I am heading over to the baby store later today so I'll keep you posted." One of my friends responds, "You find me a husband I love, and I'll get you that baby."

If you can avoid giving off a defensive and/or anxious vibe, others will be much more likely to back off. At least they will if they want to remain a part of your life. If you tell people that you are not ready to be a parent (whether it's because you haven't found a husband or it's just not the right time) and they keep harping, it's up to you to decide whether it is worth further conversation. If it's not, don't waste your time and energy. You're not obligated to explain why you don't have kids any more than a mom has to explain why she does. If you are close to those questioning you, let them know you hear their disappointment but you're making the best choices for yourself.

Know that you can't stop others from worrying about you or talking behind your back; but you can stop them from challenging, judging, or attacking you to your face. If and when they do, stop and take a deep calming breath. These people who feel so strongly they know what's best for you are being completely patronizing. You're a grown woman, for Pete's sake; just how seriously do you want to take their commentary? Tell them you will know when the time is right, and end the conversation right there.

Schedule the Mom talk: Let her know gently that she might not be a grandmother.

If your mother has been dropping hints (to say the least) about wanting to be a grandma, it's probably time to talk to her before she starts poking knitting needles into your diaphragm. The first step is to understand where she's coming from.

Plenty of moms crave the special bond that comes from watching their daughter become a mother. It's full-circle. For others the urgency to be a grandma is the desire to fill a new role. Says Dr. Karen Gail Lewis, family therapist, "Think about this as a developmental stage. Mom got married, had kids, got older, took care of her parents, and there's no next stage." You having a baby would give her that next stage called grandparenting. She also adds that many mothers find validation in watching their daughters give birth. It's a sign "that she didn't do so bad as a mom after all."

Set up a time to talk with her, with this new empathy in place. Say, "I don't know whether having a baby is going to be something I experience. I'm taking the decision very seriously and trying to figure out what's best for me. But it makes it really hard when you pressure me, because I don't want to disappoint you."

Your mom may come back with, "I'm just worried about you," or "I don't want you to miss this important step," or accuse you of making a bad decision. Let her express her feelings as long as she's being respectful to you. You can assure her, "I know this must be hard for you because you want badly to be a grandmother, but I hope you'll give me time to figure it out and respect my decision either way." This is a conversation that will likely take place several more times, but planting the seed now is a worthwhile endeavor.

 ## In case of emergency: Tune in to your baby radar.

If you're freaking out because you have reached the end of this chapter and you still don't know how far you would go to have a baby in the next couple of years, take a deep breath and answer the questions below. There are no right answers here, it is not a test; it is a guide to help you start getting more clarity for yourself.

When I think about having a baby, I feel _____
_____.

If I were told today that I would not be able to have a baby,
I would feel _____.

When I think about my life without a baby in the picture, I feel
_____.

My biggest concern about not having a baby is _____
_____.

If I found out that I was pregnant, I would feel _____
_____.

 THE COST OF RAISING A CHILD

One of the key factors in deciding whether to have a baby or not,
of course, will be whether you can financially afford it. According
to the U.S. Department of Agriculture annual report "Expendi-
tures on Children by Families," a middle-income family with a
child born in 2008 can expect to spend about $221,190 ($291,570
when adjusted for inflation) for food, shelter, and other necessi-
ties to raise that child over the next seventeen years.

3 FAVORITE MOVIES ABOUT SINGLE MOMS

1. *Baby Boom* (1987): Uber-yuppie J.C. (Diane Keaton) inherits a baby from a distant relative and has to figure out from scratch how to be a mom and create a baby-friendly environment. Hint: It's not going to be living her corporate life in the Big Apple. It does involve Vermont, an orchard, and a hottie veterinarian.

2. *Erin Brockovich* (2000): The real-life story of a jobless single mother (Julia Roberts) who becomes a legal assistant and takes on a California power company accused of polluting a city's water supply. The real Erin today is a consultant to a New York law firm and an inspiration to all of us.

3. *Waitress* (2007): In this warm, sweet tale, Jenna, a star pie-maker living in the sticks, goes into a depressed state after getting pregnant by her jerk of a husband. Although scared and anxious, she figures out how to ditch the hubby, rely on her girlfriends, set up her dream job by the end of the film, and ride off into the sunset with her newborn.

REMINDER CHECKLIST

1. Tune in to your inner voice: Do you want to have a baby?
2. Realize it's okay to feel uncertain. Look at where you are now and what works for you given your current situation.

(continued)

3. Allow yourself to feel frustration. Experiencing the intensity of the feeling will allow you to figure out what steps to take next.

4. Let yourself off the hook. Know that you made decisions that worked best for you at the time.

5. Write it down: What are your requirements for having a baby?

6. Beat your doctor to the punch. Talk to your gynecologist as soon as possible about your fertility.

7. Know your (real) alternatives. Do not get deluded by the fortysomething celebrities having babies that grace the cover of Hollywood celebrity magazines.

8. Find out where your guy stands. Know how ready he is and how long it will take him to have an answer if he is on the fence.

9. Silence the baby-obsessed. You need a one-liner that sets the record straight while making it clear the topic of baby-making is not up for discussion.

10. Schedule the Mom talk. It is time to tell your mother she may not be a grandma.

11. In case of emergency: Tune in to your baby radar.

The Slow and Steady

Definition: You hope to marry when the time is right and not cave to the massive pressure from everyone around you.

Pop Quiz

The last time someone asked you about your marriage plans, you:

(A) Laughed and said, "I'll keep you posted."
(B) Smiled and said, "Any day now."
(C) Called Security to have this person removed.

If you answered C, this chapter is for you.

LINDA'S STORY

Linda,* 33, spent her twenties caught up in a cyclone of destructive relationships that left her hurt, confused, and emotionally exhausted. She figured it was just bad luck. Over time, however, she realized she was picking men who were emotionally or literally unavailable, sometimes both. In her early thirties she started seeing a therapist to figure out why she was making less than stellar choices about men and learn how to make better choices moving forward. During this time, she stopped dating altogether (much to the dismay of certain friends and family members) and focused on why she was "picking jerks."

In addition to the hard internal work, she started taking dance classes again (a passion that had gotten lost along the way) and figuring out what made her happy on her own terms. While she missed the adrenaline rush of flirting, she refused to get distracted with flings and bad drama. When Linda finally worked through old issues and decided she was ready to date again, she almost immediately met Jim, who she knew pretty quickly was her Mr. Right. Linda and Jim have been dating for about two years and have experienced several ups and downs, such as the fact that Jim was recently laid off. Linda is thinking about going back to get her graduate degree, and they have a lot of decisions to make.

"Jim and I know we're going to get married," Linda said. "But we have so many other things to figure out first—whether I should go back to school now, whether we would relocate, could we handle a long-distance relationship if I attend school out-of-state—so it's going to be a while before we even think of a wedding." The problem, she says, is that her parents want to make sure they're both around for the wedding and are putting heavy pressure on Linda to get married now.

Stage of Singlehood

Whatever happened to living in the moment? You love your boyfriend, and he loves you. When you talk about the future, it's pretty much a given you'll be together. Maybe you've planned future vacations, discussed retirement, and imagined what your kids will be like. The bottom line is, you plan to marry each other, *just not right now*. He's fine with that, you're fine with that; it's all good. At least, it is when it's just the two of you. But it is hard to hold on to your confidence when everyone (and her sister) is telling you that you need to grow up and get married already. On your good days, you can block out the noise and remember you are doing what is right for you. But on other days, you get rattled and maybe even wonder whether you *do* have a commitment problem. Should you just tie the knot and get it over with?

The Great News

You found someone whom you enjoy being with and who hopefully treats you like the amazing woman you are. Marriages crumble all the time because couples get swept away and ignore red flags in their hasty decision to head to the altar. You, on the other hand, are refusing to rush into a wedding, even though you found a terrific guy. You want to walk down that aisle feeling confident that this is the right decision. You know there are no lifetime guarantees, but you also know that you have better chances of a healthy, sustaining marriage if you take the time now to really get to know your partner and work through potential issues.

Or maybe you're *not* sure marriage is for you. You're not against it per se—it doesn't get in the way of your personal politics or anything—but you're not particularly fired up by the idea, either. You figure you'll see how things evolve and keep tabs on your feelings. Yes, you're going to get grilled by a whole lot of people who want to know when "the big day" is coming, but there are plenty of strategies to help you handle this.

SHIFT YOUR THINKING

You'll get less heat if you're clearheaded.

If you know you're not ready for exchanging vows, but some part of you is worried you suffer from the female equivalent of Peter Pan syndrome (refusing to grow up), then take a step back. Remind yourself of the reasons you're not ready to marry and that you are fine as you are (if you're having a hard time remembering your reasons, skip ahead to the next "Write it down" exercise). While your path may be different from others', it's still the path you believe works for you. Rather than enduring ribbing, mockery, and insults, you should be receiving praise for taking marriage as seriously as you do and understanding that a wedding is more than playing princess for a day. Getting married deserves the careful thought and reflection you're giving it.

Still, there are a whole bunch of people who don't, and won't, see it this way. They get baffled when they meet women who aren't married by your age. To these folk, settling down is just how it's done, and you're throwing off the system. What kind of woman, they wonder, would choose not to marry if she *could*? If you lose your boyfriend, they admonish, you'll spend your whole life regretting that you let him get away. While their opinions and comments feel personal (why wouldn't they), the reality is that their way of thinking has nothing to do with you. Oh, and by the way, these are the same folks who will try to cajole you into having a baby right after the honeymoon if you do marry, and then another baby after the first one is born. They may even tell you that you'd better get a dog or you're downright un-American. Point being, you don't want to get caught up in their constructed vision of happiness; you want to stay grounded in your own.

What will help is being clear on why you're not up for marriage right now, and this chapter will help you get there if you're not. You'll also find strategies for dealing with people who pressure and challenge you about your decision. But first it's important to stop for a moment and ask yourself why it is that you get so agitated when someone asks you about marriage plans. What is it that *really* upsets you? We get most undone by how others perceive us when we're not sure of how we feel about our own choices. So figuring this out is the first step.

ACTION ITEMS

 Tune in to your inner voice: Why are you passing on marriage for now?

Sit in a quiet place, close your eyes, and ask yourself why marriage doesn't feel right for you at this time. Don't worry about what others might say about your answer; just pay attention to whatever thoughts and feelings surface.

The answer may be that you hold marital vows sacred and you're not going to rush it; you have some things in your life you'd like to take care of first; or you are waiting to see how your partner acts in different situations before committing to him for life. Your reason is your reason, and you don't have to explain it to others;

you just have to know it for yourself. That way you will feel centered when you start getting the grand inquisition yet again, and you'll be able to answer with no harm done to your well-being.

 ### Write it down: How would your life be different if you married tomorrow?

If you're still not sure why marriage isn't for you right now, spend ten or fifteen minutes writing in your journal about how getting married might change things ("I will feel like I sold out by marrying," "I'll be expected to be a perky wife," "Everyone will want to know when I'm getting pregnant," whatever comes to mind). When you're done, sit back and read it over, and circle the concerns that make you feel most anxious.

Many of the women I interviewed told me that they weren't ready to say "I do" for various reasons, including:

For Rebecca, a 28-year-old teacher, it is about deciding that she won't get married until all gay people in our country have the legal right to get married. She is in a serious relationship and has every intention of staying with her significant other, but she can't support the institution of marriage as it stands, particularly because she has a gay uncle she loves who can not get married legally in his state. Rebecca is happy to wait as long as it takes for her uncle to be awarded this right. As she says, "In our opinion, my boyfriend and I live a married life anyway. A lot of our friends will say, 'Oh, yeah, your wife called or your husband called,' and we joke about it."

Eliza, 30, admitted, "A certain level of heat turns up when you hit your thirties, in terms of starting a family or finding a husband or even buying a house. I do feel pressure from my family to consider having children. People are like, 'You're thirty, the time is now, and your body is ready!' But I'm not there yet. It's that simple."

June,* 45, says, "Why is it so astonishing that I might not want to get married? I have a great life—a job I love, I travel, I've got a boyfriend that I love, my own house. I am enjoying myself, so why rock the boat? Plus, we've only been together for two years. I'm not ready to commit to a lifetime with him without knowing how we will face the hard times as a couple."

Daisy, 33, said, "I want to have what my sister and her husband have in their marriage, which is a sense of we're in this together and we're a team. But I've been thinking about it a lot and looking at my old journals and realizing, I've never had a need to get married."

Do any of these answers resonate with you? Are you just happy for now with how things are? Do you have a political or personal belief against marriage? Do you sense that it's just not your destiny to marry? Did you grow up seeing your parents model a bad marriage? Again, knowing the "why" behind your reason will help you feel solid when others keep telling you that you are making a bad decision or dismiss you as a late bloomer.

Check your fear levels.

One red flag to look out for is whether you're avoiding marriage because you're afraid of repeating your parents' mistakes. Many of the women I interviewed were the first to say that witnessing their parents' divorce was brutal. The idea of going through that—and potentially doing that kind of damage to their own child—was so upsetting that they had no desire to risk marriage until they were 100 percent certain. If *this* is what's preventing you from taking the marital plunge, it's time to work through these old battle wounds with a trusted therapist. You want your decision of whether to marry to come from a place of clarity and strength, not old hurts gone unresolved.

Judith Wallerstein, psychologist and best-selling author, tracked the fate of 131 children whose parents divorced in California in the 1970s in her book, *The Unexpected Legacy of Divorce: A 25-Year Landmark Study*. She interviewed 93 of those 131 people who are now adults. Only 40 percent of those now in their thirties and forties have married. "The rest are living together, in cohabitation arrangements without marriage, at unprecedented rates," she states. Over 50 percent of them have decided not to have children, "because they believe they know too little about good parenting."

If the main model for marriage you have is your parents—who were cursing at each other and making your life hell—you clearly need new and healthier models. There's another side to marriage that you weren't exposed to, and that's being with someone who doesn't turn his back on you but rather has your back. In a healthy marriage, you can lean on your guy and you know that you are both there to support each other for the duration. Talk with friends, family, and any others you know who seem to be in healthy marriages. Ask them about the ups and downs, what they ultimately get out of marriage and how they sustain the relationship. Use their experience and life lessons to help build a new, more positive look at married life.

The same holds true for women who are afraid to commit to marriage because they've gotten hurt or have lost someone they love in *any* way (through sickness, an accident, abandonment, or another emotional trauma). If you worry about attaching your life to someone else's because they too could be "taken away from you," this is something you need to work through now because it will end up hurting your relationship whether you marry or not. Most likely, your fears will keep you from being able to sustain intimate relationships because you simply cannot be in a mature, healthy relationship if your guard is up to protect yourself. Says Frank Farley, Ph.D., professor of psychology at Temple University, "A key, often overlooked ingredient in love is risk taking, the willingness to risk opening your deepest emotional life to another person." Find someone to talk with about your feelings, do whatever it takes to heal old wounds so that you are able to risk offering your heart to someone again.

Get in sync with your significant other.

Are you clear on how your significant other feels about marrying you? Do you know if it's something he is planning for down the road, or if he's just not dealing with it at all? Maybe there is an assumption that he isn't into marriage either right now because it hasn't come up. But who's to say he's not mentioning it because he's worried about freaking you out? Or maybe you're assuming you'll get married someday but he hasn't given it a moment's thought? It's also possible, of course, that he's not a fan of marriage, period.

Said one 29-year-old, "I assumed my boyfriend wanted to marry me. He was always making little comments about where we'd retire when we grew old and what we'd do with our grandchildren. And then right before the Christmas holidays, he broke up with me and said he was moving out. It was shocking given his comments about our future. Why did he bother? It's not like

I was pressuring him in any way to marry me. If I learned any-thing, it's do not assume you know what a guy is thinking in terms of your relationship."

Do not make any assumptions that you know where your man stands. If he is someone you want around in your life (or at least for the foreseeable future), then have that discussion with him. Tell him where you are now and what you're hoping for down the road, and ask him what he wants in terms of building a future. There are just too many stories where someone spends years with his or her partner in the belief that marriage is the obvious path, only to find out it was never going to happen for the other per-son. Hopefully, you two will find out your plans align; but if they don't, this is the time to find out so you can make an informed decision about whether to stay with him.

If it turns out that your significant other is ready to marry now or even soon—and you're not there yet—be clear with him on why you're not ready. If you love him and want him to wait, it is not enough to ask him to sit by until you're ready. Help him to understand why you need more time and assure him, if you can honestly, that your need to wait has nothing to do with how much you care about him. Don't put off this discussion until he's already feeling insecure; talk about it as soon as you know that he's even thinking about marrying you. You owe him that.

Speaking of letting things drag on, a word of caution from Stephanie Klein, well-known blogger of Greek Tragedy (http://stepanieklein.com/greek): "Many people I know stay in relationships, for many years, waiting for some epiphany." She goes on to say that "with the fear of loss and regret governing their decisions, they decide, 'Okay, fine. We made it this long. Guess we'll get married.'"

Her advice: "You shouldn't be engaged if you aren't rip-roaring ready to be married the very next day."

Compare notes with your guy.

If you are on the same page with your significant other in terms of wanting marriage someday but not yet, that's optimal. Knowing you are in a similar position right now, why not use each other as a support team to face outside pressure? There's a good chance your boyfriend is getting his fair share of grilling over popping the question to you from his own family and friends. Yes, even guy friends tease each other mercilessly about this kind of stuff, especially when it's coming from his friends who are already hitched. Talk to your boyfriend; ask him if he's feeling outside pressure to pop the question. If he says yes, ask him how he handles it, and whether he has any tips for you. Hey, why not add some new tactics to your repertoire?

Even if your boyfriend says that he isn't dealing with outside pressure, it's a good idea to share with him what you are experiencing anyway. He may not be able to commiserate but he can certainly listen and empathize, and get your back the next time he sees someone coming at you. This is your partner, married or not, so allow him to give you support and help ease some of the tensions.

"I came home crying one day," said Dina,* 27, "because everyone at my lunch table at the office started asking why my boyfriend and I were not married and which one of us was dragging our feet. Usually I just blow off these stupid comments, but it really upset me on this day. When I got home I told my boyfriend, and I let him know that I didn't want him to say anything bad about my office mates, I just wanted to vent. He was awesome, he just let me talk it through and I felt so much better. He gave me a hug and that's really all I needed. That one day made us closer."

Create a canned answer to "When are you getting married?"

There will be times when it's just you in the room getting grilled, no backup. It's especially annoying when the perpetrator is someone you hardly know and/or who has no business asking you in the first place. Why should you have to explain to your second cousin once removed why you're not marrying your boyfriend right now? After all, you don't ask her about her love life or why she stays in her marriage, right? Well, sadly, you can't stop others from asking, but you can have a stock answer ready so you never feel taken off guard.

One woman told me her answer is, "I will get married the day that Barry Manilow joins Metallica"; another woman told me she responds, "You'll know when I know"; yet another said her favorite answer is, "It's up to how the stars align"; and another tells people, "We'll get married the day people stop asking us about it."

Develop your own signature line. It can be saucy, straightforward, funny, sweet; it should feel like you. With your signature line in tow you don't have to worry about being caught off guard by someone demanding to know why you're not married yet. Who hasn't had a conversation that went something like this:

Acquaintance: "I haven't seen you for a while. How are you?"

You: "I'm good—"

Acquaintance: "—So are you and your guy setting a wedding date?"

You: "Not yet . . ."

Acquaintance: "What are you waiting for?"

You: "Umm, well . . ."

With a one-liner at hand, you can easily turn the conversation around without spending any emotional energy, not one ounce, feeling upset at being put on the spot. There is no scrambling for answers and defending yourself, and repeating the scenario again and again later, in your head, wishing you had said or done something differently. By the way, don't feel like you have to come up with one perfect line or you've failed. Try one out a few times, see how it feels. Adjust it or change it as necessary.

Get more personal with those you love.

It's one thing if an acquaintance asks you about getting married. It's a whole other thing when you're asked about it by somebody who truly cares about you and is trying to understand you better. These people are entitled to something more than a flippant, dismissive one-liner. When you are clear on the reason, it will be no hardship to explain it to someone you care about. They might not understand it fully, but knowing you have taken the decision seriously should be enough to satisfy most of them, even if they don't like your reasons. If they're not satisfied, too bad.

"I remember telling my family that I am nowhere near being ready to marry," said Angela,* 31. "At first it didn't go all that well because I felt defensive and they were picking up on that, so the conversation started spiraling out of control with everyone weighing in on my business. A few days later I called everyone back together and apologized for yelling. Then I explained to them as a group that I am not ready to get married. Maybe I will be someday, maybe I won't, but I just want them to be happy that I have found somebody I love and who loves me. All of a sudden there was much more acceptance because I came to it from a grounded place. I would definitely recommend that approach if you're thinking of talking to your own family or close friends about not wanting to marry."

It may not go so well. Instead of supporting you, it's entirely possible that your family and friends will rally around trying to get you to change your mind. They may even go the route of staging some horrible type of intervention. Don't get rattled. You know what is best for you right now. Take a deep breath, and tell them that you are comfortable with your decision and they need to let go of the topic once and for all. The date of your wedding is now off-limits.

Do they really think you're going to be peer pressured into marriage? And what kind of family victory would that be? The idea of marrying to get your family off your back, while appealing sometimes, is hardly a solid plan. I like what Joshua Estrin, a life coach and author of *Shut Up! and Listen to Yourself* said: "You know tying the knot will lead to a noose that will hang you when you only want to get married because all your friends are married, you're afraid you will never find anyone, your mother tells you that you should be married, and/or you believe this other person will make you feel complete."

Schedule the Mom talk: Let her know your wedding won't be in this calendar year.

Your mom is probably experiencing the same relentless grilling about your relationship that you are. You'd better believe that her friends are talking about their daughters' weddings and asking her when you were going to settle down. There's a pretty good chance that your mom is feeling like she has to defend your choice and isn't sure how to handle it. She may be asking you about your marriage plans because she herself is feeling beaten down by outside pressure.

So instead of getting on her case the next time she asks you about your wedding, tell her that there are no plans right now but that you understand this might be hard for her. If you're feeling generous, ask her about the anxieties and fears around you not marrying right now. You shouldn't do this if it feels like it's at your own expense. But if you can swing it emotionally, you may greatly benefit from allowing her the freedom of releasing her anxieties. Remember, though, it's not your job to fix her fears, just to listen if you can.

It may help her to know that you have been experiencing the same type of outside judgment, and how hard it is, and what you've done to help alleviate it. Believe it or not, she may be inspired by your survival tactics and even take on some of them to use on people who are giving her the inquisition. Ask her if she has any suggestions for you. Having been around the block, she might know some healthy ways of getting people off your back. In fact, it just might help her see that it's time for her to defend you rather than stay on the offense.

Find your support team—and stay connected.

You are not alone in your decision to not marry right now, in spite of the fact that it may feel that way sometimes. This is especially true when you don't know other women in the same situation, who are also waiting. When you start feeling all alone in your thoughts, visit a singles forum and participate in discussions with women around the world who are dealing with similar struggles.

It may also help to log on to single women's blogs and read about the ups and downs the blogger is experiencing. There are some amazing single women writing authentically about being unhitched in a marriage-obsessed culture. Sometimes this feeling of connection is really all you need to feel understood and normal. A few that I like:

- Onely: Single and Happy (www.Onely.org): helps reverse popular conceptions of what it means to be single in our culture.
- Quirkyalone (Quirkyalone.net): geared to people who "enjoy being single (but are not opposed to being in a relationship) and prefer being single to dating for the sake of being in a relationship."
- Singletude (http://singletude.blogspot.com): a positive, supportive singles blog about life choices for the new single majority.

Also, make a point of planning more events and outings with friends who you know are not going to pressure you, so you can relax. I'm talking about the people who either think it's refreshing you're not interested in marriage, or couldn't care less about it. Either way, it barely comes up when you guys hang out. Maybe these people haven't been superclose friends in the past, but you always liked them. Go out of your way to connect with them now. (That doesn't mean you have to ditch your close friends who are gunning for you to get married, just that you need counterpoints to them.)

"I thought it would be easiest hanging out with single women when I first moved to this city," said Joan,* 28, who was in a committed relationship but not ready to marry. "I figured they would support me, while married women would think I was judging them because I didn't want to marry. But as it turned out, I met some married women who thought it was great that I was taking my time before getting married because they knew how hard it could be after saying 'I do.' In fact, a couple told me that they wished they had spent more time getting to know their husbands because they might have made different choices. They made me feel brave instead of freakish."

Journey to your people.

The idea of rushing to the altar is actually a very American attitude. In Nordic countries and Southern Europe, cohabitation has been on the rise for a long while now. Finding couples who are perfectly happy cohabitating for years and years (even forever) is no big deal.

Betsey Stephenson, an economics professor at Wharton, explains this is true in part because "there's not much of a legal distinction between being married and not being married in Europe." In America, for example, the government taxes the household, whereas in Europe the government taxes the individual. That means many people in the United States who marry get certain benefits and provisions that makes marriage a better economic choice. "In Europe, most of the countries have moved away from that. So you are seeing people who are less likely to get married in these other countries, because it just doesn't seem that important."

Her research and relationship partner, Justin Wolfers, added, "I'm from Australia, where cohabitation is very common and is a widely accepted alternative to marriage. So for the first nine years of being together I thought that we had the most natural relationship in the world [being an unmarried couple], and there was nothing odd about the fact that we weren't formally married."

Why not consider visiting one of these countries during vacation time and getting a taste of being odd girl *in*. You'll feel positively normal and won't have to explain your relationships to anyone you meet. It could be just the break you need from being on the defensive all the time. Your best options: Sweden, Iceland, Denmark, Greece, Italy.

But if you don't have the time or money to travel, you can at least take comfort knowing that in other parts of the world, nobody would blink an eye at the fact that you're not thinking about heading to the altar right now. In the meantime—while you're living in your marriage-centric country—you can use the strategies of this chapter to raise your confidence so naysayers are less likely to get to you. Honor the inner Swede inside you and continue to follow the path that is best for you.

 ## In case of emergency: Get out of Dodge.

If you're feeling overwhelmed by the pressure to get married, grab some alone time ASAP. It's easy to get caught up in the frenzy of people telling you that you better hurry up and seal the wedding deal before your guy changes his mind. "You're throwing away a great thing," people will insist, "you're blowing it." What you want to do is scream, "I'm not throwing away anything, so mind your own business!" and delete every person you know from your cell and e-mail contact list. Instead, head directly to a favorite retreat, sign up for an outdoor day trip, or visit an out-of-town friend who supports you. The time away will give you a chance to regain your perspective on why you are setting your own pace.

 GET OUT OF CREDIT CARD DEBT

If you or your partner is in any kind of credit card debt, this is the time to fix that before getting hitched and mingling finances. Marrying into a partner's debt is a really crappy way to start a marriage. So if you're in credit card debt, like a whole lot of other folks right now, here is the first step you should take, according to Gerry Willis in her article "Struggling with Credit Card Debt" on CNNMoney.com: If you've lost your job or can't make your credit card payment for any other reason, call your lender and explain the situation. "The sooner you contact them," she says, "the more willing they may be to work with you. More and more credit card companies are willing to negotiate. Realize that they're not being charitable—they're just trying to get what they can out of you."

⭐ 5 FEMALE CELEBS WHO PAVED THE WAY

Let's have a moment of thanks for the glamorous, bold women who hadn't married by age thirty, even as paparazzi questioned their every relationship step. Here are five of my favorites, along with inspiring quotes from them.

Penelope Cruz: "I don't believe in marriage. I believe in family, love and children." (*Psychologies* magazine, UK, 2009)

Cameron Diaz: "I think women are afraid to say that they don't want children because they're going to get shunned." (*Cosmopolitan*, 2009)

Oprah Winfrey: "With every experience, you alone are painting your own canvas, thought by thought, choice by choice." (Oprah Winfrey's Power of Giving website)

Jennifer Aniston: "If I'm the emblem for 'This is what it looks like to be the lonely girl getting on with her life,' then so be it. It's fine. I can take it. I can make fun of myself. And I'll bring it up as long as the world is bringing it up." (*Elle*, 2009)

Selma Hayek: "For many women, marriage is only about needing the world to know that someone desires them enough to say, 'Here's a contract to prove that I love you and will commit to you for the rest of my life.'" (*Woman's World*, 2006)

REMINDER CHECKLIST

1. Tune in to your inner voice: Why are you passing on marriage for now?

2. Write it down: How would your life be different if you married tomorrow?

3. Check your fear levels. Decide whether you're avoiding marriage out of fear.

4. Get in sync with your significant other. Don't assume he's in the same place as you are until you discuss marriage.

5. Compare notes with your guy. Ask your boyfriend for backup when you're dealing with others pressuring you.

6. Create a canned answer to "When are you getting married?" That way, you won't feel cornered when you're asked yet again.

7. Get more personal with those you love. Close family and friends may benefit from you explaining why marriage isn't for you.

8. Schedule the Mom talk. Tell your mother that marriage is something you're planning on—but not yet, and not anytime soon.

9. Find your support team—and stay connected. Surround yourself with some women who are in the same situation you are and can relate to what you're feeling.

10. Journey to your people. If you can, take a trip somewhere where cohabitation is the norm and not the exception.

11. In case of emergency: Get out of Dodge.

12

The Trailblazer

Definition: Married life is not for you, so you're going to need a compass with a new path toward happiness.

Pop Quiz

When you picture yourself as an older single woman, you:

A Imagine planning Margarita Mondays with your senior friends.

B Can't totally picture it, but trust you'd make a good life.

C Join more online dating websites in a state of wild panic.

If you answered A or B, this chapter is for you.

CECELIA'S STORY

Cecelia, 36, is a Mexican-born actress who divides her time between Mexico and the United States. She currently has a serious boyfriend but no intentions of wedding him. For her, marriage is definitely not in the cards because she thinks the idea "is archaic, an antique form of two people relating."

She went on to say that marriage is just about having society recognize that two people are in a relationship and can now pro-create. She could see the point during certain times in history, "but you no longer have to be married to have children, so who needs it?" Not her, she hopes to stay with her current boyfriend but has no intention of walking down the wedding aisle with him.

Stage of Singlehood

You like being unmarried in spite of the fact that no one seems to be able to wrap their brain around that idea. You have no problem asking for a table for one; you are the first to sign up for a solo travel adventure; and you relish being able to make spontaneous plans on the weekends. Sure, you might have a day where you wake up missing intimacy, wishing you were dating more, or feeling sad about your biological clock, and you are also open to changing your mind about marriage if it happens, but you can't picture it. There would be no problem at all if you lived in a bubble. But, unfortu-nately, in our culture there is still a race to get married, and the finish line (a wedding) seems to signal everyone that you've won; you're normal. So where do you fit in if you're not even *interested* in that finish line? Setting your own path is exciting, but it's also lonely and filled with outside pressure and judgment.

The Great News

You are basically living the life right now you actually want. How many people can say that? Okay, fine, it's not always picture perfect (there's no such thing) and you may not be winning any life-approval awards from some people. But let's look at the big picture: you're creating a life that works for you. Huge props to you for realizing that staying true to yourself means passing on the conventional route and opting to take life as it comes. For the rest of your days, you'll be able to draw on this ability to carve your own path—in spite of what others think—and no one can take that precious gift away.

Of course, the other good news is that you have an abundance of freedom and can do what you like without having to check in or report back to anyone. If you want to stay out late with the girls on Friday night, go ahead. If you want to take a sabbatical from work and volunteer at a coffee plantation in Costa Rica, no problem—as long as you can organize the details. You call the shots to your own life. Opting to remain single also means more freedom to date whom you like without the pressure of figuring out if your guy is husband material. He doesn't need to be; you can just enjoy spending time with a man because he's nice to be around.

SHIFT YOUR THINKING

Recognize the pull of the race.

Although the majority of women I interviewed cited "freedom" as the best part of being single, that didn't mean they necessarily felt free all or even most of the time. During the three years I conducted interviews, I don't think there was one single woman I spoke with who didn't feel at least some pressure to marry.

Plenty of women, in fact, said life would be just fine if they didn't have to deal with people who could not comprehend a woman possibly being happy on her own. In spite of the fact that there are more singles today than ever (in 2007, *The New York Times* published an article titled "51 Percent of Women Are Now Living Without a Spouse," stating it was probably the first time there were more unmarried women than married women in the U.S.), being unmarried is still a problem to be fixed for many people; and women are still asked to explain why they're single and whether they are doing anything to remedy this social "dilemma."

If you fit into this category of "single and fine if everyone would back off," you know what I'm talking about. You know the headache of being cornered at parties and reunions by an obnoxious someone who pulls you aside and asks in a stage whisper, "You're such a lovely person! How can it be that you're still single?" You know how demeaning it is when a colleague exclaims in front of everyone in the lunchroom: "I have a friend who did speed dating last month, and he said it wasn't nearly as bad as he expected." And, God forbid you look disinterested, because you know what's coming next: "Have you thought of trying that? What do you have to lose?"

What makes these awkward moments worse is the understanding that the real message is (a) you can't possibly be happy if you don't marry, and (b) you don't fit in and we're all uncomfortable so you better do something to fix it. No matter how confident and self-assured you are, it's hard to feel like you're making top-notch choices when relatives and colleagues keep trying to "fix" you so you can *really* be happy. The thought of spending years restating ad nauseum that you *are* happy can be daunting.

Considering this pressure, it's hardly a surprise that women of all ages often describe feeling caught in a giant "race" to the wedding altar. The problem here is that this proverbial race doesn't make sense for you because you're not even heading in that direction. This chapter is about learning how to quit the race so you can set your own course, and in your own time. That's the life, after all, that will bring you the most pleasure—and the one you deserve.

ACTION ITEMS

Realize you're on familiar turf.

Remember back in sixth grade when you knew that if you didn't have the right pair of blue jeans or watch the right TV shows or listen to a specific band, you'd be deemed a loser? By around seventh grade (now it's probably fifth grade, but don't get me started) there was the sense that if you didn't make out with a guy or wear the right bra size—not too small, but not embarrassingly big—you wouldn't make the cut. Let's not forget down the line when you felt excluded if you didn't get your driver's license the first time you took the test or didn't get accepted to the "right" college. Then there's finding your first apartment, a brag-worthy job, and on and on. At practically every stage of life there is a push to keep up with those around you and a compulsion to yell, "Everything's just fine here!"

As you're well aware, many people believe there's also a right way and a wrong way to schedule your adult life. The right way:

"Get married, have baby, then have baby number two. You're having a second baby, right? No minivan? Are you getting a dog? Okay, phew. It's all right, she's getting a dog!"

I love how one 38-year-old single attorney put it: "We are told how to be happy from our religion, TV, movies, books. It always looks the same: marriage and babies! But what if you want to carve out your own happiness and follow another path? You're practically named a delinquent. It's one of the hardest things to do, to forge your own path." For the record, this single says that it may feel like hard work but she has built a good life for herself made up of satisfying work, salsa lessons when she can fit them in, close relationships with her family, and "awesome friends who appreciate my sense of independence." If her colleagues at work would stop asking her why she's still single and who she's bringing to the Christmas party, she says her life would be even better. She added, "There are plenty of days when I don't care what others think, but it's hard when the obnoxious comments come on a day when I'm already feeling blah."

Appreciate that you've made it to where you are just fine without necessarily achieving the perfect bra size, right pair of jeans, or driver's license on the first try. Do any of those past milestones even matter to your life? If you can keep a clear mind—and retain your sense of humor—you will begin to see the silliness of these meaningless races.

Go ahead and quit.

Okay, you know exactly who and what events make you worry that you're lagging behind in life. This is the perfect time to take a deep breath and say, "I quit the race." Better yet, shout it out loud. Because once you pull yourself out of the race, and you refuse to let others force you back under any circumstances, you no longer have to take part in the madness. You set your own pace and your own agenda. As for other people worrying about whether your speed and direction are off, let them (hell, you can't stop them anyway).

Granted, it can feel weird at first to veer in a new direction after so many years of assuming there was only one way to go but, as you'll soon see, it is freeing. If you're not part of the race, you're not worrying about who is sprinting ahead of you or whether others are lagging behind. You can even saunter over to the roses across the way, the ones you would have missed had you rushed by, and take a whiff.

Grace, a 36-year-old event planner, quit the race when she canceled her own wedding. Here she was engaged to a fiancé who was perfect on paper: handsome, smart, professional, Korean (like her)—all the things she was looking for in a partner. But in the midst of planning her wedding, Grace started to realize that she wasn't happy. At first she denied it, hoping it was normal jitters, but as the months went by, it became more and more undeniable that there was a major problem.

"I went to the grocery store one night," she said, "and I saw all these women who were coming home from work and they were tired and they had kids and I was like, 'I can't be that tired yet. I can't give [my life] up yet.' I then went by a playground and I saw these moms in the minivans driving their kids to soccer or whatever else and I just freaked out. I just could not imagine myself being in that place at that time." Grace canceled the wedding.

She admits that there were costs to her decision. In addition to the emotional devastation she caused her fiancé, her family even now remains disappointed in her choice, which saddens Grace during family gatherings. Relatives simply can't understand why she "threw it all away" when she was so close. But Grace says she knows she made the right decision. As she told me, "I am at peace with this. It's taken me a few years to get through it but yeah, I think life is really, really good now."

Shield yourself with a one-liner.

Hopefully, you've got family and friends cheering you on as you chart your own course as a single woman. They love you for who you are and trust that you know how to make good choices for yourself. Unfortunately, not *everyone* will support you in spite of your new confidence, so I recommend having a one-liner for times when, out of the blue, you are put on the defensive. Maybe it's your grandmother who wants to know whether you are *really* trying to find someone; maybe it's your coworker who keeps sending you online links to dating sites; maybe it's your guy friend who says, "I just don't know why guys don't seem to like you." So come up with a pithy answer. That's why it's important to come up with one now, when you don't need it.

A few possibilities: "Thanks for asking. I'm happy with my life right now." "I'm on hiatus from talking about relationships. How are you doing?" "I've got to tell you, I'm good with being single." Maybe it's something sarcastic or funny or straightforward. If it's really going to work, it's got to feel natural and sound like *you*. If you're not sure about your one-liner, practice saying it a few times out loud to your dog, your plants, your reflection in the mirror. Tune in to how it feels (ignoring the fact that you're talking to an inanimate object).

It's also essential that you are clear and calm when you deliver your one-liner. Hopefully, the listener will get the point and drop the badgering; if they don't, refrain from getting baited into explaining your single status for the umpteenth time. Tell the person, instead, you need to refresh your drink or make a phone call or fly a Lear jet across the country. Women who are in the midst of being lectured to like they're under age ten sometimes forget that they don't have to stand there and take it. You've done nothing wrong. Having your one-liner in stock means knowing you're never going to have to sit through a condescending lecture again.

Educate those you're close to.

It's one thing if some annoying relative you see twice a year makes a crass comment about your future role as a spinster. It's a whole other thing when it comes from your sibling or close colleague or a friend you see regularly. Maybe they make jokes about your being single that are "in good fun" (uh-huh, fun), or attempt to set you up with any man who is single and breathing, or make a mental sport out of analyzing why you're still single. Most likely, these folks truly don't mean to hurt you, and think they are helping you—but let's face it, they're not succeeding and they need to stop. This is not the time for a one-liner; this is the time to help them understand the impact of their words.

The next time one of them makes a snarky or jokey comment, take that person aside, look the person in the eye and say, "I know that you'd like to see me married, but it's not what I want for myself and you need to respect that," or "I need you to stop making comments about my love life. It hurts my feelings." You don't need to go on and on, just state your point in a firm tone. Hopefully this person will own up to his or her action, on the spot or soon after.

For Tracy,* 38, it was time to deal with her older sister, who frequently made comments like "There's Tracy, always the bridesmaid!" and "When are we going to see you walking down that aisle already?" Finally, Tracy sat down with her sis and told her calmly that those "jokes" offended her. She explained that she is happy being single right now but that it's hard when people she loves tell her that she shouldn't be. "At first, I think my sister was embarrassed and she didn't say much," Tracy said. "But then a few days later, she called me to say she was probably making those jokes because she sometimes feels jealous, and fantasizes about being single again. I had no idea!" The sisters were able to get their relationship back on track, and an even better track than before, according to Tracy.

If the person you're talking with heard everything you said and then presses to know why their comment was rude, why you aren't willing to be set up, how you're going to make it in life if you don't get married—let them know. They may be genuinely struggling to figure out what is wrong about their behavior and how you can live a lifestyle so foreign to them. Let them know that you're satisfied with the choices you are making too.

Keep calm if the conversation nosedives.

If the discussion takes a downward spiral (like the other person tells you that you're being a drama queen and overly sensitive), keep your cool. In her book *The Power of Positive Confrontation*, Barbara Pachter, an expert in business communication, says, "Don't get defensive back. The defensive person may not have the skills or the same ability to treat and consider others that you have. Don't apologize or justify your feelings. Your goal is to try to engage the person in discussion." She suggests telling the other person, "I'm surprised by your response," which can help that person see they're acting inappropriately. Or you can always say, "I'd like to talk to you more about this when you calm down." Then wait for them to bring it up again. If weeks go by, you can always pick up the phone and say, "I'm sad about how our conversation ended at the party. Can we try again?"

The people who genuinely care about your well-being are going to make an effort to understand you or, at the very least, support you. And as for those "friends" who refuse to see your point or accept your approach to life, you probably want to examine whether they are adding significant value to your life. You wouldn't consider dropping a girlfriend because she told you she was getting married or is pregnant, right? You deserve kindness and respect from your friends, assuming it's what you offer them. Also, don't forget to be appreciative for those friends of yours who boost your spirits and applaud the fact that you're doing what's right for yourself.

Schedule the Mom talk: Explain why marriage isn't for you—and it's not her fault.

First things first: tell your mother you would like to talk with her about your thoughts around being single. Ask her for a good time to chat, rather than launching into a soliloquy. The conversation is going to go a whole lot smoother if she feels she isn't being attacked. If possible, meet in person. If you live long-distance, it's okay to pick up the phone. Do not under any circumstances e-mail because there's an excellent chance you'll misunderstand each other and end up not speaking for months.

To start on a good note, says relationship expert Dr. Karen Gail Lewis, assure her that you love her and appreciate her willingness to listen. Tell her that you sense it's important to her to see you married and you'd like to understand why it's so important to her. Allow her to respond without interruption. She may tell you she has been dreaming of your wedding for years; or she worries about who will take care of you when she's gone; or she fears your being single reflects a flaw in her mothering; or she may have another reason. Remember that her comments have nothing to do with *you* or how incredible you are; they are based on her own hang-ups. So unclench your fists and keep breathing. If she says something horribly rude, tell her, "Mom, I'd like to hear your thoughts but I won't sit here and be insulted."

Now let your mom know that you heard her by parroting back what she just said ("Mom, I hear you are concerned about [fill in blank] and wish that I would marry so you could stop worrying"). Don't try to explain why she's dead wrong or being silly; her feelings are her feelings. Once she's finished, assure her that you are happy being unmarried and it is a lifestyle that works for you. You can add, "I'm sorry this makes you worry because I love you, but I have to live in a way that's right for me." You may even want to let her know your decision is not a bad reflection on her parenting; if anything, you appreciate her raising you to be courageous and chart your own path. Lastly, let her know that you would like her support. At the very least, you need her to stop pressuring you to marry.

Hopefully, this talk will end in a supportive hug (if you're in the same room together). It may not. In fact, you may have to revisit this conversation several more times. That's okay, because this is a conversation worth taking the time to get right. Whether it went perfect or not, treat yourself to a reward—a new haircut, a walk somewhere pretty, a book you've wanted to pick up—for taking this bold step.

 ## Tune in to your inner voice: So where do you go from here?

Find a quiet spot, close your eyes, and ask yourself what your life might look like now that you've decided to head off the beaten path. What can you picture making you most happy?

 ## Write it down: What goals can you set to get there?

Spend twenty to thirty minutes writing in your journal things you'd like to accomplish for yourself in the upcoming year and maybe in the next few years as well. Since you may not have milestones as obvious as "wedding" or "give birth," it may be helpful to have this list of life goals.

It can feel strange for goal-oriented women to intentionally pull out of the race because where does that leave you? What are you heading toward? Some of you may leave room for the possibility of wanting marriage and kids at some point down the road. Others may know in your heart that "the picket fence" dream isn't for you. Maybe you fantasize about a life that includes exotic travel; setting your own schedule; moving across the country, or exploring the world. Maybe it's a calmer, tamer life that just flows at its own pace.

If you're envisioning possibilities this moment, that's fantastic. But for those unsure about where you're heading, remember that it's better to be uncertain than to be on a crowded path that you know is going the wrong way. Spiritual teacher Eckhart Tolle got it right when he talked about the futility of worrying about the future: "You can always cope with the present moment, but you cannot cope with something that is only a mind projection." If you are not able to tap into what life will look like in five, ten, twenty years . . . that's fine; you may be better off anyway. By continuing to stay in the moment, you get to choose a life that is never dependent on Mr. Right waltzing in.

Elli, 32, assumed she'd end up with her longtime boyfriend. She had to find a new map after they broke up four years into the relationship. "My boyfriend suddenly moved out of my overpriced New York City apartment," she said, "and it ended up leading to one of my best moments. Two years after he left, he announced he was engaged to someone else. I was surprised that I was not hurt or jealous. After pondering this, it suddenly occurred to me that I had my own fairy tale I was living: for two years, I had actually been able to afford the full amount of my apartment rent—$3,500/month—on my own because all the time I had put into my relationship had now gone into my small business and not only was I happier, but my business was taking off and I was *still* doing everything I had a desire to do. I realized I had made *my* life, and I have never been more content running my business, being able to afford a wonderful apartment, and surviving the grueling streets of New York City as a one-woman army. Of course, dating a man eleven years my junior helped pass the time as well."

Round up fellow trailblazers.

The next step is to find other singles—if you don't know some already—who are reinventing their lives as they go. This kind of support can be a real blessing since you can boost each other's spirits and congratulate each other when you take a risk. These women don't have to be your best friends; they have to be supporters who help you feel connected to a larger community.

To find fellow trailblazers, seek out an activity where you'll likely find other adventurous singles. It may be a soccer league that meets a few times a week after work, or a "cooking for one" adult-ed class, or a rafting trip for solo adventurers. Relationship expert Jerusha Stewart suggests going to dating events, because the women are always infinitely cooler than the men, and they often swap phone numbers with one another before the night is over. (I can vouch for this myself.) Don't get dismayed if you don't end up loving any of the women you met in your new group. You're not obligated to stick it out with them, so try something new. Or look on Internet forums and chat rooms specifically for singles.

You can also find like-minded compatriots on bookstore shelves or the pages of Amazon.com. Look for memoirs and biographies about women charting their own course. They don't have to be stories about single women, specifically; they can be accounts of anyone who ditched the conventional life and trekked out on their own. Check "Travel," "Memoir," and "Entrepreneur/ Business" sections to locate reads on inspiring role models. A few of my personal favorites: *The Late Bloomer's Revolution* by Amy Cohen; *Eat, Pray, Love* by Elizabeth Gilbert; and *Expecting Adam* by Martha Beck. They're different in style, tone, and content, but each author reveals with candor the ups, downs, setbacks, and triumphs of finding her own way when everyone insisted she was "doing it wrong."

Quit the race again, if needed.

You may be feeling upbeat and confident about living your life in this new intentional way; you've met fabulous friends who are as unconventional as you and you're happier living in the moment. Then one day something happens and—*bam!*—you find yourself thinking that it's really hard being a pioneer and life would sure be a whole lot easier if you just got married like everybody else. Does this mean you're back where you started? No. We all have setbacks and it's important not to punish yourself if and when you find yourself getting caught up in the race again. Just because you know that being single is right for you does not mean you won't experience occasional self-doubt and insecurity. You're not a machine.

Lara, in her late thirties, for instance, said that as embarrassing as it is, Valentine's Day made her feel "like crap" every year for a long time. In spite of knowing she was just fine being single, she'd freak out on the heart-themed holiday, knowing that "my eight or nine friends around the country were married and celebrating a romantic night with their husbands. I'd think, maybe I should rush out and try to find a date. Do I go find a bartender to sleep with? What do I do?"

There are likely to be plenty of incidents that tempt you back into the race as well: Mom sending you a newspaper announcement about a couple getting married (moms who are reading this: stop mailing these; they are in no way helpful) . . . A slew of friends giving birth in one summer . . . Wishing you could cheer up an ailing parent by walking down the wedding aisle. You may think in these moments, "Oh no, I let myself get yanked into the race again. I failed." But you are not in the same place as when you first pulled out of the race. Now you understand that you are better off moving toward your own destination—even when this road-less-traveled gets rocky. You're better equipped to deal with inane comments that you're going in the wrong direction ("You're going to end up all alone!" and "Don't come crying to me if you are lonely"). It may sting for a moment but it won't keep you from doing what's right for you. The point here is *not* to get to a place where there are no triggers; the goal is to make sure that these triggers don't prevent you from living your best life.

 ## In case of emergency: Keep a note of reminder.

Write a letter to remind yourself about why being single is a better alternative for you than being married right now, using as much detail as possible. What do you find appealing about being single? What opportunities are open to you as a single woman that wouldn't be if you were married? What would you have to give up if you were married? How does it make you feel when you think about getting married right now? Reading this letter when you feel shaky will help get you back in touch with your needs when you're feeling unsure.

 PREVENT IDENTITY THEFT

As you're trailblazing a new path and taking advantage of the finer things in life (whether it's a night out with the girls or a rafting trip to Cambodia), make sure you don't fall prey to identity theft. This is when someone acquires a piece of your personal information without your knowledge and uses it to commit fraud. According to the United States Department of Justice, one of the most common identity theft tactics is when criminals listen in at public places when people give their credit card number over the telephone to a hotel or a rental car company. Make sure you find a private place to talk and cover your hand over your mouth. Be extra careful with your bank or a credit card statements, Social Security number, and checks—shredding them instead of leaving them out with the trash (where someone can easily Dumpster dive and nab them). If you do happen to have your personal info stolen, close your credit cards and bank accounts immediately and then open new ones.

8 REASONS HAVING YOUR OWN PLACE BEATS LIVING WITH A HUSBAND

1. You don't have to tiptoe around your guy when he's pissed off. The mood in your house is whatever mood you're feeling.

2. You can eat as weirdly as you want. There's nobody to give you judgmental looks when you snack on a toasted bagel for the third night in a row. Over the sink. In your undies.

3. Splurge in whatever you like. Longing to purchase expensive light-blocking blinds or upgrade your cable plan? Go ahead, it's coming from your savings account and you don't need permission.

4. The style of your place reflects you. No need to showcase a shot-glass collection from cities around the United States; go ahead and hang that Georgia O'Keeffe poster without threatening anyone's manhood.

5. Peace and quiet. After work, you can throw on a John Legend CD rather than enduring *The Ultimate Fighter* blaring from your TV set.

6. You can tweeze your eyebrows, bleach your upper lip, or use nostril-burning depilatories on your inner thighs without locking yourself in the bathroom.

7. You don't have to entertain his friends at your place—the guy with the rank-smelling socks, the guy who farts every time he stands up, or the guy who goes around yelling lewd jokes.

8. You're assured a peaceful night of sleep since there's no one to roll onto your hair, elbow you in the face, or keep you awake with torturous snoring.

REMINDER CHECKLIST

1. You're on familiar turf. Remember that you likely have a model for dealing with massive peer pressure.

2. Go ahead and quit. Make the intentional decision to pull out of the race to the finish line.

3. Shield yourself with a one-liner. You can repackage the same answer over and over to the question of why you aren't married.

4. Educate those you're close to. For close friends and family, you may want to explain your reasons for not wanting to walk the aisle.

5. Keep cool if the conversation nosedives. If the discussion gets ugly and judgmental, it's time to walk away.

6. Schedule the Mom talk. Tell your mother you're taking a different path—and it's not her fault.

7. Tune in to your inner voice. So where do you go from here?

8. Write it down: What goals can you set to get there?

9. Round up fellow trailblazers. Find like-minded single women so you can boost each other up and celebrate your successes.

10. Quit the race again, if needed. Don't beat up on yourself if you find yourself doubting your decisions on occasion; it's hard to walk the less traveled path.

11. In case of emergency: Keep a note reminding you of why you choose not to marry.

Conclusion

What Screenings Have in
Common with Being Single

After almost three years of working on the documentary *Seeking Happily Ever After*, it was time to screen it for friends, peers, and total strangers. My producer, Kerry David, and I shaped more than 110 hours of footage into a feature that was less than an hour and a half, and we needed a fresh perspective. At this point, we were in "rough cut" mode, meaning we had our story mapped out but didn't have in place the bells and whistles of cool graphics, our final music, proper audio, etc. We wanted feedback on the story, the heart of the movie.

To that end, we hosted about a half dozen screenings in less than two weeks, and asked viewers to give us specific feedback on what was and wasn't working. They did not hold back, believe me. We listened to hours and hours of thoughts, suggestions, criticism, and both good and terrible ideas. Most of the people who screened the doc sent e-mails the next day with even more feedback and still more comments; we agreed it was great they were still thinking about it, but it was a lot to take in. Overall, Kerry and I were pleased with the process. Viewers found the women in this film relatable and honest; they connected with our main character emotionally; and they said they learned a whole lot about a complicated topic they were deeply interested in. Most important, everyone wanted to talk (and talk some more) about it.

But there was criticism to deal with, as each and every person who watched it had strong feelings about what was missing. Academics wanted more cerebral information with charts and graphs and interviews with historians; plenty of others could have done with fewer experts and even more personal stories ("I just want to hear from other single women, and that's it"). Married people wanted to hear from other married people; men wanted to hear from more men; everyone wanted to see themselves reflected in some significant way. Everyone wanted their voice and their ideas expressed.

While these screenings were extremely useful to us, they were emotionally draining. In many ways, this film represents my deepest, most personal beliefs, and I found it difficult, sometimes painful, to listen to all of the suggestions without defending my choices—even if I had asked for honest feedback. I had to refrain more than a few times from shouting, "No, you don't even get it!" and "Why don't *you* try making a movie?!"

It did help knowing that most of the viewers came from a good place of wanting this movie to fly; they cared about it. This made it easier to hear their thoughts without getting rattled or even losing, it. But I spent a lot of time sitting by myself after each screening, taking deep breaths and asking which criticisms felt useful, and which would truly help this project. Thank God, my producer and I had become close friends and could also talk each other through this process and keep each other grounded.

I also realized something interesting: These screenings paralleled the experience of being a single woman today. Everybody has ideas about what you should be doing, what you should stop doing, and what would be so much better for you if you would just listen. Of course, unlike me, you haven't asked for the no-holds-barred feedback like I did. Still, given the parallels, I want to share what I learned in the big picture. Most of these messages and insights are scattered throughout this book, but I think they are worth repeating in one place.

Keep an open mind (even when you want to leave the room).

There were people who were able to see things about the movie that weren't working, which I wasn't able to see because I was so close to the project. As one example, I hadn't considered how a certain scene might offend or confuse someone. There were assumptions I made about how a scene would play, and it just didn't work. (For instance, one man we interviewed for the doc said his girlfriend broke up because she was in PETA, and he "ate cows, and she didn't like that I ate cows." I laughed out loud every time I heard this; no one else did. No one. It had to go.) When I asked viewers what might make a particular scene better, some came up with excellent solutions we ended up using. Or we came up with our own ideas on how to fix it and felt grateful they had pointed out the problem at a time when we could fix it.

While you are the best expert on yourself, that doesn't mean you should shut yourself off from other people's perspectives and feedback entirely. For better and for worse, there are people who can frame things in a certain light or share a specific insight that may illuminate something important—even life changing—for you. They might tell you that an aspect about your behavior is getting in the way of you connecting in relationships; or they might alert you that you are starting to lose balance in a profound way. Who knows what it will be? The point is, you don't have to take it to heart or use what they say, but it's worth hearing out people who are absolutely on your side and want to help you be your best self. So much of dealing with constructive criticism rests on knowing you can trust the messenger.

If it's not constructive,
trash it (and forget it).

In one of the screenings, a thirtysomething guy told me that he found certain pivotal scenes in the movie boring. When I asked him why—was it the length of those scenes, or the topics covered, or the characters in them—he said "they're just not interesting." *Gee, that's helpful; thanks!* In the meantime, these particular scenes played very well with most of the screeners, so I decided it wasn't worth tuning in to what he was saying or trying to better understand his point. Or perhaps it was that he was just rude. I thanked him for his thoughts and then pretty much ignored what he said for the rest of the night. The cost of listening to him wasn't *worth* hearing a potentially helpful point.

When you're single, a lot of people have a lot of ideas (and, frankly, a lot of put-downs) that just aren't constructive ("Men don't like smart women, so you should dumb it down a bit," or

"You don't dress sexy enough. That's your problem"). If you're in a sensitive place, it can easily rattle your confidence. Even though you know intellectually the person made a stupid point, it can still seep in. Don't let it. Avoid wasting your time analyzing thoughtless comments and dismiss them for the obnoxious opinions they are. It's one thing to remain open to feedback from people who you respect, and a whole other thing to allow insensitive jerks to wreak havoc with your self-esteem. You are under no obligation to listen to these people; you owe them nothing.

You really do know yourself best (in spite of what others think).

All those who watched the documentary brought to it their own personal frame of reference: their trials and tribulations, their own relationship anxieties and insecurities, their life lessons learned, and the pivotal experiences that shaped them. All of these things clearly informed their perspectives on the doc. Each viewer felt like an expert because everyone has experienced love, being single, and heartache. That didn't mean they knew what was best for the overall project. Their experiences are worthwhile and important for them, but that didn't mean their ideas and insights should be in this film. Not every single perspective and voice can, or should, make it into a film under ninety minutes.

In the same way, those you are close to cannot possibly know better than you what will make you your best self. People make a habit of saying you should do exactly what worked for them ("Oh, I met my husband on Match.com. You have to try it!" or "Forget all about online dating, it was a big waste of my time"). While their heart may be in the right place—wanting you to be happy—it's just ridiculous to assume you should repeat exactly what someone else did. You need to carve your own path and remember there is no one set of instructions you should be following. Your own inner voice—the one you have been accessing throughout this entire book—will keep you on track.

Remember where you're heading (so you don't get lost in all the noise).

I wrote a mission statement for myself before I started the screenings: "Your goal is to create a film that reflects your beliefs, feels true to you, and encourages women to think through their choices and explore their options." I knew I wouldn't be able to make people love my film or give me standing ovations or even agree with what I'd said. I could only articulate my honest personal vision, say what I wanted to say, and hope that it resonated with my audience. Whenever I lost sight of this (oh, and did I), I went back and reread my mission statement.

The same will hold true for you. You are going to have to find, through trial and error, what decisions work best for you, and know that you cannot control what people think of them. It doesn't matter whether you're for marriage, against it, want babies, don't, like being coupled, hate it, whatever. In the end you have to figure out what is right for yourself and let everyone else just deal with it. You may not get the huge cheers and applause you were hoping for from certain people, but that's beside the point. You can feel good about knowing you are strong and brave enough to commit to making the healthy but unpopular choices for yourself. It is truly courageous to live this way, and the payoff is feeling good about running your own life.

Make sure you have a friend (who really gets you).

What made the screenings particularly tough some nights was running the sessions alone, given that Kerry was off doing her own screenings on the other side of the country. It would have been easier to do them together, I think. Still, after every single screening, Kerry and I would hop on the phone and debrief. We'd talk about what certain people said, why we thought they said it, whether it was helpful or not, and what we were going to do about it, if anything. We discussed our own responses and whether certain things came out right (or drastically wrong). If someone said something ridiculous or even hurtful, we'd cheer the other up and offer sympathy, or crack a joke to lighten the mood. Having this support system in place was essential for this ride.

You need a support system too. Maybe it's a friend you can call on after a bad date; or when you're feeling like a failure because your baby sister just got engaged; or your mom just lectured you yet again about getting out there and trying to meet a guy. Know ahead of time who you're going to call in these scenarios and who you absolutely shouldn't call (the married friend who can't relate to any of this or the jealous friend who wishes she were single). It may be that you have to "coach" a close friend a little by saying something like, "I have to tell you what happened and if you could just listen, I would totally appreciate it. I don't even want an answer, I just need sympathy." Or "Please just tell me I'm going to find someone." Good friends shouldn't be expected to guess what you need; but they should try to give it to you once you have told them and if they can, and vice versa.

But there is one major difference...

All of us are rough cuts, works in progress. We keep growing and fine-tuning as we go along trying to find our way. Unlike a film, however, in which the story eventually becomes "locked" into place—our own story keeps on veering off in unexpected directions.

Yes, the idea of locking in our story—at a time when everything is going smoothly—is pretty appealing. It's also pretty boring. The whole point of life, as I see it, is the adventurous and sometimes wild ride. I recently overheard someone saying, "Life is too good right now, I'm afraid something bad is going to happen," and the answer is, "Yep, it is." But then something great is going to come along again. The only thing that's predictable is that your life will be fairly unpredictable.

How do you deal with that?

That's for you to decide. You can certainly opt to freak out, and many people do. But the whole point of this book is to give you the tools that you need so you don't have to. By owning these tools, you don't need to panic if you get lost because you can bank on the fact that you will find your way again; and when you're right on target, you know to take time to appreciate how it feels and to review how you got there. Learning how to navigate the ups and downs of being single (or of anything, really) comes from practice— and from seeing over and over again that you know how to steady yourself when you get disoriented. You take a deep breath, re-check your internal compass, and set off again with a new plan. No beating up on yourself, no shame.

Navigating the ups and downs with *confidence* is not something that happens right away; it's not like learning how to flip a pancake or figure out a new computer program. Over time you will collect a history of these moments where you were able to get yourself back on track, and this collection of moments will become your go-to model. Instead of thinking, "Ugh, I can't stand how I'm feeling!" you can get to "Oh, this place is not doing it for me, but the same thing happened when fill-in-the-blank and I was able to get through that just fine." Once you have this model in place, no one can ever take it away from you. It is your gift for life.

In the end, getting lost and finding your way are both part of the same journey. That's why the fairy-tale ending (the kiss at the wedding, or any other moment that's supposed to mark the moment of your *arrival*) is so ridiculous and annoying; it's static, a useless model. For better and worse, we know we'll receive our share of good and bad news for as long as we live. Knowing that we are prepared for both of these—that we have the resilience to handle the full journey—*that* is Happily Ever After.

ACKNOWLEDGMENTS

First and foremost, I want to thank "all the single ladies" who trusted me with their intimate feelings. I know it wasn't always easy and that the feelings weren't always "pretty," but I also know that sharing them will inspire readers to seek their own path.

Thank you, Laney Katz Becker, my agent, who is smart as a whip and ridiculously hardworking, and boldly gets the job done. Gabrielle Moss, my editor at Tarcher, I appreciate that you understood this book intuitively and fought for it—the fact that you're wise and hilarious is the icing on the cake. Thank you, Brianna Yamashita, my publicist at Tarcher, for your enthusiasm, and all the other fabulous folks at Tarcher for bringing this book to life.

Bobbi Silver (aka Mom), I've learned so much from watching you continuously reinvent yourself and opting always to reach for joy. Jules Spotts, my stepdad, thank you for your waving pom-poms and soulful conversations.

Kerry David, filmmaking partner extraordinaire, I am grateful to you for being rock solid—as a partner and friend.

Thank you to "my girls," who nourish my well-being: Betsy

Block, Kathy Bloomfield, Jacquie Boas, Wendy Diamond, Lisa Frattini, Tanya Michaelson, Shelley Ruff, Pam Templer, and Susanna Bray.

A shout-out of love and appreciation for the Silvers, as well as the Chasin crew.

As for my fellow Coves—husband, Ezra, and daughter, Risa—you continue to be my safe harbor.

INDEX

ABOUT THE AUTHOR

Michelle Cove is the director and a producer of the feature-length documentary *Seeking Happily Ever: One Generation's Struggle to Redefine the Fairytale* (www.seekinghappilyeverafter.com). She is a regular guest columnist for Single Minded Women (www.singlemindedwomen.com) and editor of *614: HBI eZine*, an online magazine that explores hot topics for Jewish young women. Cove is a coauthor of the national bestseller *"I'm Not Mad, I Just Hate You!,"* a new understanding of mother-daughter conflict (Viking, 1999), which was featured on several national talk shows, including *The Oprah Winfrey Show* and *Today*. For the past fifteen years, she has been writing and editing for national magazines and blogs, among them *Psychology Today*, *Skirt!* magazine, Women & Hollywood, *Mother Earth News*, *Girls' Life*, and *FamilyFun*. She lives in Brookline, Massachusetts, with her husband, Ezra, and daughter, Risa.